C000136809

ENTREPRENEURSHIP

A Guide to Success for Entrepreneurs and Aspiring Entrepreneurs

By

Thomas D. Mathieu

First Edition

Copyright 2018 by Thomas D. Mathieu

Introduction

If you have read some of Robert Kiyosaki's inspirational material on success in life and business, you are aware of a concept he calls the ***cashflow quadrant.***

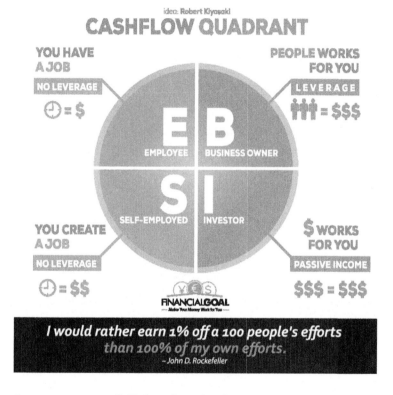

Image courtesy of all-free-download

While the idea is Kiyosaki's—in that he created it to segregate the different types of incomes and careers—the general ideas behind the concept are neither new nor foreign. In fact, we can go as far as to say that the cashflow quadrant is how many successful people have been able to achieve the success they now have.

Take the example of Warren Buffet. Most people know that

the 'Oracle of Omaha' bought his first stock at the age of 11 thanks to his interactions with the traders at his father's small brokerage firm and the money he had saved from working his paper route.

If we relate this to the cashflow quadrant, we can see that this stock investment placed Buffet in investor (I) quadrant. What many do not know is that like most people, Buffet started his life in Employee (E) quadrant. First, he worked a paper route, which is why he had money to invest at the age of 11. This made him an employee. The other thing is that as a teenager, Buffet also worked odd jobs such as washing cars.

As a high school sophomore, Buffet used his savings to buy pinball machines that he then placed at various local businesses. The business was a boom and before he was 15, he had already generated about $6,000.

Again, looking at the cashflow quadrant, we can see that his investment in the pinball machines made him a Business Owner (B quadrant) long before he was 16 years old. From there, the story of Warren Buffet's rise to a net worth of over $83.3 Billion has been an adventure.

The cashflow quadrant is how you achieve success in life and business. It's the strategy used by all millionaires and billionaires in the world. The quadrant moves anticlockwise.

It starts at **E** where you are an employee— because no matter how great you are at a specific business, you need hands-on knowledge and above all, capital. From there, it moves to **S** for self-employed where you create a job for yourself. In this case, you work in the business yourself and without your input, you would stop earning.

It then moves to **B** for business owner where you own a business that employs people and leverage their skills to grow your business to scalability and profitability. From there, as your business grows and your net worth improves, you move to **I** for investment quadrant, where you invest the money you generate in other profitable businesses and stock.

Success in life (we are talking specifically about financial success) is about moving through the cashflow quadrant as rapidly as possible with the idea being to get to the I quadrant so that you do not have to work for money. Instead, money works for you.

The best way to get to this point is to become a business owner, which at heart, is what we call being an entrepreneur.

This guide is about how you can achieve entrepreneurship success irrespective of the business you start. The guide is not going to discuss businesses you can start. That would be too assumptive—assuming that the businesses discussed can work for all. Instead, the guide is going to outline entrepreneurship principles that, when applied, will help you create value-driven business that generates wealth for you and the people whose skills you leverage so that in the end, you have money to invest.

Let's begin.

Table of Contents

Part 5: Preparing a Business Plan

Chapter 17: How to Create a Business Plan for your Business

The Rules

The Essential Elements of a Business Plan

Chapter 18: How to Create a Marketing Plan for Your Business

Situational Analysis

Matching Product Features to Benefits

Demographic Analysis

Chapter 19: Competitive Analysis

Identifying Direct and Indirect Competitors

Identifying Competitive Advantage

Chapter 20: Creating Your Marketing Budget

Your Marketing Goals

Marketing Tactics and Strategies

Part 6: Operations Management

Chapter 21: Introduction to Operations Management

What is Operation Management?

The Functions and Importance of Operations Management

The Essential Qualities of an Operations Manager

Chapter 22: Facets of Operations Management

Inventory Management

Part 1: Entrepreneurship 101: Everything You Need to Know About Entrepreneurship

We live in a world where although our level of education is better than that of say those in the 1990s, we are also experiencing massive population growth. The population growth in itself is not bad; what makes it bad is that as population grows, governments across the world cannot keep up with the growth spurts, which is why most developing countries are in crises.

If you look at most countries—developing or otherwise—you will note that the gap between the rich and poor is very big. You will also note that in most countries, unemployment is at an all-time high as governments struggle to keep up with job demand and colleges and universities continue to produce new ones each day.

The high levels of unemployment mean higher levels of crimes such as muggings and to some extent hunger and starvation as many families across the world struggle to live on under $1 a day. Higher levels of unemployment inequality have also led to instability and insecurity, which perhaps explains why crimes such as cybercrimes, human trafficking, and credit card theft have become commonplace.

Yes, we are more educated and will probably even live longer than those who came before us. Despite this, however, despite the educational system doing a great job of producing graduates in specialized disciplines, it has substantially failed to produce job creators/entrepreneurs. In fact, we can go as far as to say that the educational systems of the world teach graduates how to look for jobs instead of creating them.

While this is not bad in itself, when you consider that governments across the world are struggling to create employment opportunities, it becomes bad because it means that if people like you and I do not create jobs by being entrepreneurial, our economies will constantly suffer and take a beating.

This guide is a call to action to you. It asks you to take up the mantle and, instead of waiting for your government to do it, or blaming politicians for their biased laws and corruption, start creating jobs.

In this section of the guide, we will cover what it means to be an entrepreneur, someone who sees solutions to problems and creates businesses out of those solutions, how entrepreneurship compares to self-employment, and the core traits every entrepreneur needs to have to achieve massive success.

Above that, the guide teaches you the skills you need to have (and how to apply them) to venture into entrepreneurship successfully.

Chapter 1: Understanding Entrepreneurship

Most people are of the belief that entrepreneurship is about making it to the list of top X or Y or having such a massive amount of wealth that you become a subject of discussion in the media and gossip blogs. They believe that entrepreneurship is about being a rich millionaire who lives in a posh estate, drives expensive cars, and travels to exotic places.

To some degree, entrepreneurship is about these things. However, wealth is but a product of entrepreneurship, not its aim. In fact, although wealth and fame often follow successful entrepreneurship, they may not happen and their happenstance does not qualify or disqualify one as an entrepreneur.

We can blame this confusion on the simple fact that the term entrepreneurship has various definitions. Being great at anything demands a level of understanding of that which you want to pursue which is why to become a great entrepreneur, you have to understand what it means or should mean.

Succinctly put, entrepreneurship is about risk: it is about noticing/perceiving needs and then taking the risk to create a business solution around the need. What does this tell you? It should tell you that an entrepreneur is someone so attuned to societal needs that he or she perceives business opportunities in the simplest of things.

For instance, before computers became something that we can now carry around in our bags, they were bulky things that only universities, banks, and government institutions could afford, maintain and keep. From this state, Steve Jobs, the exuberant co-founder of Apple Inc. saw a need for home computers and set out to create a solution: because he knew that someday, the world would need less bulky computers that could fit in homes and that anyone could operate. That is how Apple Computers, one of the most progressive, profitable, and solution oriented businesses started: as a solution to a problem.

Above being able to recognize opportunities, needs in societies or communities, entrepreneurs must also be willing to go out of their way to take risk. Although measured one—assuming the entrepreneur maps out the solution and its implementation—the risk is still there because starting any business is a risk in itself because no matter how perceptive the greatest entrepreneur is, conceiving an idea that meets a need requires a fair amount of risk taking.

Above that, we can also say that entrepreneurship is about organizing a business enterprise in the most responsible of ways to ensure that even as the entrepreneur bears the non-insurable risk that comes with conceiving goods and services that satisfy a need, he or she does so in a way that proves profitable.

To this end, the entrepreneur takes charge of directing human and material resources that complement the business objective. This may mean raising capital or finding the right talent that fits specific spots in the business.

In general, an entrepreneur is someone who does the following:

- Perceives needs

- Conceives goods and services to satisfy needs

- Bears the risk

- Organizes factors of production

- Manufactures and markets the products

- Innovates

- Manages the business

- Identifies, selects and acquires key resources

- Obtains all the necessary licenses, permits, and approvals for doing business

However, while all the above fit in the repertoire of an entrepreneur, entrepreneurship is more than that; to most of those who venture into it, it is a calling, a call to action, to do something that will impact and change life for the better—for the entrepreneur and those around him or her.

Chapter 2: An Entrepreneur's Lifecycle—A Hero's Journey

Finding Joe is one of the most influential documentaries ever created.

https://www.youtube.com/watch?v=-CpsYGc1PVo

In it, Joseph Campbell, a deceased philosopher and professor of Literature at Sarah Lawrence College, describes something he calls the Hero's journey. Yes, the term sounds very vague and something you are likely to see in a fictional book or movie (instead of a non-fictional book about starting a business).

We have stated above that entrepreneurship is a journey, a risky one at that because on top of conceiving the idea or service, an entrepreneur also bears all the risk that comes with starting the enterprise.

That journey, a journey where you know not what the future holds but are sure of the power you hold inside you and how it can positively change the world around you, the power to know that if you don't heed the calling, you will live a comfortable but fake life, that is the Hero's journey.

In Campbell's tale of the Hero's journey, the journey starts with an inner calling. When you look at the lives of some of the most influential and successful entrepreneurs the world has ever seen, you will note that the start of their entrepreneurial journey started with an inner calling, something so powerful that no one in his or her right mind would ignore.

In some cases, this inner calling is a revolutionary idea. In other cases, the inner calling is a disarrayed life and the need to quit the work you are currently doing to pursue something greater (a sort of like The Monk Who Gave up His Ferrari kind of thing).

As Campbell calls it, the "call to adventure" is so strong and right that it confounds all logic and sense. However, when the hero in the story (you are the hero in your entrepreneurial story) heeds the call to action and enters into the unknown (what we are calling taking risks), the "symbolic death" attunes you to the universe that then creates doors when none existed earlier.

The symbolic death we are talking about is the change that comes with taking the risk. For instance, when you quit the job you hate so much and instead decide to pursue your acting career or dream, some of the habits you have been practicing will die; that is the symbolic death.

The entrepreneurial journey is a lot like the Hero's journey.

The first thing that makes it so is that like the hero's journey, entrepreneurship is a journey of self-discovery. Other than the risk that comes with taking the plunge into the unknown, when you heed the call, the entrepreneurial call, you encounter challenges, "dragons" that you must defeat for your quest to become triumphant.

In most cases, especially at the start of your entrepreneurial journey, the dragons are fear of the unknown, of losing your investment, of losing your time, and of societal perceptions of your decision to stop living a mediocre life, and to start pursuing something larger. In the Hero's Journey, Campbell calls this slaying the dragon.

The connection between the hero's journey and entrepreneurship is that entrepreneurship is a calling, a way of life embarked by only those who are willing to heed the call and embark on the journey. By conceiving business ideas that solve a problem in the entrepreneur's immediate or larger community, the entrepreneur also changes the lives of others around him or her.

The other connection is that as the hero's journey is full of trials, hard work, and confusion, an entrepreneur's life is the same on many levels. As an entrepreneur, you have to overcome a lot of challenges, fears, and confusion. Since putting a product/service out to market and marketing in the most effective, profitable way is not easy, you will also have to do a lot of work.

Another parallel between entrepreneurs and the Hero's journey as described in Campbell's book, The Hero with a Thousand Faces, is that like the hero in every story, movie, book, or song, an entrepreneur undertakes the journey, the journey to conceptualize his or her grand idea in writing and then actualize the same idea in reality.

To understand how the hero's journey relates to your entrepreneurial journey, we need to look at the hero's journey in stages:

In actuality, every entrepreneur—yes, even the likes of Steve Jobs, Bill Gates, Richard Branson, Mark Zuckerberg, and any other entrepreneur you can think of—starts in what we call a conventional market. The conventional market is the ordinary life tied to traditions and customs—in the case of an entrepreneur, that is a conventional market, products and services.

Because the entrepreneur is creative—otherwise, he or she would be unable to create a viable solution to a problem—he or she is up to the task of overcoming everyday challenges and by so doing, visualize, and envision the possibilities available.

Like the hero in the journey, an entrepreneur is someone who is willing to depart from conventional living and thinking and from the comfort of security of a job and the known world. Like the hero in the story, an entrepreneur is someone who is willing to pay the price, to take the risk, which is what the hero's journey calls "heeding to the call to adventure."

As an entrepreneur, when that call comes, you must be ready to ask yourself, "what if?" "What if I quit my job and started the business I have been contemplating starting for the last 5 years?" "What If I could solve this problem by offering this solution?"

The "what if" question is a very powerful question that opens you (and other entrepreneurs and heroes) to an endless sea of possibility to change conventional thinking and stories and perhaps create something new that diverges from the conventional—perhaps a new product or service, or even a new way of doing things.

As hinted at earlier, the call can come in many ways. It can come as a personal decision driven by the need to find fulfillment in life, or something else such as passion, economic difficulties, loss of a job, or other types of changes within and beyond our control. As hinted at earlier, the initial stage is very trying because at that point, you are battling the fear of the unknown. In this initial stage, although the call to action is very strong, you are also free to reject the call, which means committing to the status quo.

When you accept the call, you cross the line into the unfamiliar, which is what we called metaphorical death. This crossing signifies the burning of bridges in that once you cross the threshold, once you make the decision to quit your day job for instance and venture into entrepreneurship, there is no turning back. This stage complements the "what if" stage in that now that you have chosen to heed the call to action and crossed into the familiar, you will be asking yourself tons of questions on how to overcome the many challenges that will be on your path.

In this stage, you will ask yourself many questions with some of them being "What if I implement this idea in this way?" "How can I implement this idea and communicate the ingenuity of the solution to potential buyers and investors?" Like stories of most heroes, once you venture into this face, you, the entrepreneur, will need to work hard through the trials, failures, challenges, and new discoveries as you move towards creating a feasible product and business.

You will have to find new allies, friends, and supporters who see your vision and are willing to help you actualize it. Overcoming these challenges and presenting your vision in the most logical and adept way is what will make you a leader in your chosen field.

You now know what entrepreneurship is, who an entrepreneur is, as well as how journey-like the prospect truly is. Now that you know this, let us go a step ahead and detail the qualities every entrepreneur must have:

Chapter 3: Qualities of an Entrepreneur

To implement the initiatives we mentioned in chapter 1, an entrepreneur needs to have specific character traits. A quick study of the most successful entrepreneurs you know will reveal a real and tangible connection in terms of qualities and characteristics.

To this end, the following are the most outstanding qualities of an entrepreneur:

1: Self-discipline

Self-discipline is a central character trait in the life of all entrepreneurs. Without this one character trait, it would be impossible to take an idea from the conceptualization stage to the successful implementation one. Self-discipline is so important in life that whether you are or are not an entrepreneur, your success in life, career, and business depends on your ability to control yourself.

As an entrepreneur, you must discipline yourself to do that which you need to do when you need to do whether you like it or not. If you can do this one thing, if you can manage to do this, to overlook your urges and temptations and do what is necessary, you will achieve success in all areas of your life, including entrepreneurship.

To become self-disciplined enough to achieve entrepreneurial success, you need to exercise self-responsibility, self-mastery (of self and emotions), self-direction, and above all else, self-control because in most instances, the difference between successful and non-successful entrepreneur is the former's ability to take the necessary action irrespective of situation.

Coincidentally, it is not that successful people love doing the hard things. That is not that case; in fact, successful people do not like doing the same things that unsuccessful people do not like doing. The main difference, however, is that successful people, in this case, successful entrepreneurs, choose to do these things anyway because they know that doing the very thing they hate is the very thing that will help them achieve that which they want.

2: Integrity

Integrity is another important entrepreneurial character trait. Integrity is important because in business, men and women who keep their word and mean what they say (and say what they mean) command respect. To earn this respect, integrity is one of the most valuable qualities you need to develop.

Whatever you do in business and in your personal life, practice the qualities of honesty and truthfulness. Always say what you mean and mean what you say. Always keep in mind that those you interact and do business with will treat your word as your bond and tie your honor to it.

For instance, when you say you will deliver some goods at a specific date or make payments by X date, go out of your way to keep your word and if doing so is not possible, communicate the same to your business associates. This way, you will create trust, something without which no business can thrive.

In fact, we can go as far as to say that, how much success you achieve in business will greatly depend on the people that trust you. Only by being trustworthy, which requires that you be a person of very high integrity, can you get talented people to rally behind your mission. Trust is also the only way to get investors on board especially when you are dealing with a trying time.

Always remember that your integrity determines your character.

3: Persistence

Persistence, the ability to keep at something until something gives, is another common character trait amongst all successful entrepreneurs. Persistence and character are two peas in a pod and none can exist without the other (no wonder both qualities are so important to overall success in life and success in business in specific).

While there are many ways to develop persistence (being discipline and self-controlled is one of the best ways), the most logical way is to prepare for setbacks, roadblocks, failures, and disappointments in advance. This will ensure that when these things happen in your actual life and journey to business and life success, you have the ability to move past them in the most fluid of manners.

Great entrepreneurs are never quick to give up when things fail to go their way. Take the example of Thomas A Edison. A great quote by this man that invented the electric bulb goes something like this, "I have not failed. I have just found 10,000 ways that will not work."

Rumor has it that Edison tried 10,000 times before he successfully created the first iteration of the modern day bulb on the 10,001st try. If he had given up on the 10,000th attempt, perhaps he would not have been the one to create something used by so many people in the world.

Now that you are getting into entrepreneurship (or are an entrepreneur), resolve right now to purge giving up from your mindset. No matter what happens, no matter how many times you fail at achieving that which you want to achieve, DO NOT GIVE UP. Learn from the failures, disappointments, and adversities, pick up the pieces, and continue moving forward in earnest. Successful entrepreneurs are those that persevere when others have given up.

4: Sense of Direction

Like most worthwhile undertakings, entrepreneurial success is a lot like a treasure quest in that, to achieve it, you need a sort of map. In this case, the map is your business plan and its implementation plan. To implement your business plan, you need a clear sense of direction. You need to know what to do and when to do it to ensure your business does not become like every other business that struggles to survive day after day.

A clear sense of direction is what ensures that, instead of concentrating on short-term problems that only appear important but are not, you can keep your eyes on the big goal. It ensures that you create an effectual plan for the future of your business and map out how you intend to drive your business into scalable profitability.

Developing a clear sense of direction demands that you set clear objectives and targets for yourself as a business proprietor and for your business in general—set goals for the specific area of your business venture. Having a clear sense of direction makes you responsible to not only yourself and your business, but also to the people working for you/under you. Having a clear sense of purpose and direction also ensures responsible coordination in all that you and your people do to drive the business forward and into profitability.

5: Action (Initiative) and Decisiveness

Of the things we have discussed about being an entrepreneur, one of them is that all entrepreneurs need to be ingenious, resourceful, and alert so that they can quickly detect opportunities that exist in the environment and take advantage of them just as fast.

Decisiveness and the ability to take action are two of the most important character traits an entrepreneur can have. When your intuition says there is a very worthwhile opportunity in X or Y market, you must be able to make a decisive decision on whether to get into that market and then take action immediately because if you are not quick to implement worthwhile ideas, someone will beat you to the punch.

Obviously, being decisive and quick to take action does not mean you should be quick to pull the trigger all willy-nilly; that is not the case. You must think all your decisions through in the fastest, most conventional way possible and from there, follow through on the decisions you make.

Seeing that the business world is constantly changing, to achieve entrepreneurial success, you must be quick to make decisions and then disciplined enough to follow through (take action) on decisions made. The quicker you can get feedback for action taken, the quicker you will move past mistakes, and the closer you will get to the business success you crave.

The ability to make decisions quickly and then turn those decisions into action is the very thing that will determine how fast you move past mistakes and, coincidentally, how fast you achieve success.

If you develop these character traits, you will triumph in business (and life) because above all else, you will develop the right mindset, a mindset of trying. Successful entrepreneurs are the ones who try more. The more you try—of course by trying, we mean trying different things (trying the same thing repeatedly expecting different results is the definition of insanity)—the faster you will move towards success, business, life, or otherwise.

Now that we have discussed these character traits, before we start outlining the steps you need to take to develop your business, let us compare self-employment and entrepreneurship.

Chapter 4: Self-employment vs. Entrepreneurship

At the start of this guide, we discussed something we called the cashflow quadrant that, as we stated, has four segments. To live a financially free life, you have to move through the four quadrants (in an anticlockwise manner) as fast as possible and get to the investor quadrant.

When you start working for yourself, i.e. generating an income not tied to employment, you become what we call self-employed. Some of the most common attributes of self-employment include the following:

- The scale of operation is usually very low and made up of the owner and one or two other workers. The entrepreneurial role here is very low while management skills are almost zero.

- Most, if not all the work is done by the owner based on the special skills and ability in the particular area.

- The income generated at this level is also very low. In most cases, individuals go into self-employment as result of their inability to secure a job in the formal sector.

- Entry and exit into self-employment is very easy as there are virtually no barriers. Skills and capital requirements are low and do not constitute a major barrier.

- Capital for self-employment is usually easy to accumulate from personal savings while skills are also easy to acquire from apprenticeship.

While self-employment is great (great in that on the cashflow quadrant, it moves you a step closer to the right quadrants), you should never confuse self-employment and entrepreneurship: the two are very different. Not all self-employed persons are entrepreneurs but all entrepreneurs are self-employed.

Are you Self-employed or an Entrepreneur?

From the above discussion, one thing we can say about entrepreneurship is that entrepreneurs involve themselves in the complex business operations in terms of size and use of technology. Unlike the self-employed, entrepreneurs also assume greater risk, are more innovative (in that they are responsible for the continual creation of new products and services for the business), and often times need better managerial skills.

If you examine the U.S. business scene, you will note an abundance of small businesses owned and run by people who consider themselves their own bosses. Small businesses are an important part of the economy. However, and as we have stated above, while small business owners are experts in their fields, not all small business owners are entrepreneurs. The truth is that most of these people, even those who have employees, are self-employed.

The great difference between an entrepreneur and someone who is self-employed is that if the small business owner fails to go to work, the business is likely to take a hit and to some extent, stop operations; perhaps not on the first day, but eventually.

To ensure this does not happen, the self-employed person has to invest time and energy into running the business and keeping the customers provided for. In most cases, the compromise is that by doing this, the person compromises his or her needs as well as those of the business.

In self-employment, there exists a great disconnect between the admirable commitment, the built pipelines and customer bases, and the systems to manage and grow the business and its various elements to a point where the business can work without the daily input of the creator.

Because a business owner is most often the technical brains behind the business, when facing overwhelming business demands and tasks, he or she has to perform business services and activities. For instance, a self-employed baker will bake; a graphic designer will design, while a freelance writer will write for his or her clients.

While the technician aspect of any business is an important element none of us can overlook, to the self-employed, this comes at a compromise: that of managing, which is what an entrepreneur does best as he/she seeks to grow and strengthen the business. In other words, while a self-employed person acts as a technician who delivers the work needed by customers, an entrepreneur concentrates on managing the technicians who deliver the work to the customers. This creates room for growth because by creating this segregation, the entrepreneur can concentrate on the things the business needs to grow.

The real difference between entrepreneurship and self-employment is not the workload. Entrepreneurs work just as much as the self-employed, perhaps even more. The main difference is the difference in mindset and the way the two see business and the world in general.

The greatest example of this is that in most cases, a self-employed person tries to be a jack-of-all-trades within the business. He or she will try to be the baker, the marketer, the sales person, the deliveryman, and everything else a bakery needs to run profitably—this is primarily because in the mind of the self-employed person, no one can do the job better.

Entrepreneurs know and understand that above all else, they cannot be everything the business needs; they know they cannot do everything, which is why they concentrate on what they do best i.e. innovation and management, and delegate the rest to the capable hands in their payroll.

These are the main differences between an entrepreneur and a self-employed person. Having looked at that, let us move the discussion forward:

Chapter 5: Entrepreneurship and the Economy

Earlier on in our discussions, we mentioned how governments across the world are struggling to create employment opportunities for their citizenry and how high unemployment levels are hindering economic growth (as well as peace and governance) in most countries around the world.

The other side of this is that while governments are indeed the largest employers (when you consider all the civil servants and government employees such as teachers, police officers, firefighters, etc.), business such as Apple, Microsoft, and many other businesses owned by entrepreneurs are central to job creation.

Entrepreneurs are vital agents of social and economic transformation and change. They, for example

- Create jobs for themselves and for others by establishing new businesses.

- Raise the level of production in the economy through harnessing and utilizing resources more efficiently

- Are innovators, developing new products and services, adapting existing technologies to local realities, and adding more value to goods and services.

- Are engineers of economic development through the creation of wealth and stimulating the economy thus pulling out of any decline or recession.

The Role of Entrepreneurship in Stimulating Economic Growth

Most governments have some form of entrepreneurship program. This is because entrepreneurs are central to the growth of any country, which perhaps explains why many countries see them as national treasures that need all the support they can get. Entrepreneurs play a very vital role in the growth of a society especially when it comes to the growth of the economy.

Among other things, entrepreneurs are central to the growth of the economy because:

1: They create new businesses

As we have discussed, entrepreneurs are innovative thinkers who create innovative solutions to societal problems; they are trailblazers who create new goods and services that can have a viral effect on societal growth and the economy.

Take the example of Apple Inc., a company that Steve Jobs and associates started at his mom's garage, which now employs over 47,000 people in the U.S. alone. A company such as Amazon has over half a million employees.

The point here is that by creating new goods and services, entrepreneurs stimulate economic growth not only because of the jobs they create, but also because the goods and services they create stimulate and support other sectors.

Take the example of the IT industry. In most countries, only a few companies are responsible for the massive development. In a country such as India, the IT industry developed out of a backend programmers' hub established by a few companies in the 1990s. Soon after, and as the industry grew in leaps and bounds, it benefited many other sections. For example, out of the IT industry grew other businesses such as hardware providers, call center operations, computer education, infrastructural development, internet providers, and many other businesses that went on to grow, flourish and thus create employment.

As you can see from this discussion, entrepreneurs are central to economic development more so because their businesses create employment opportunities for thousands if not millions.

2: Source of National Income

The businesses started by entrepreneurs are very central to the growth of a society not just because of the jobs they create, but also because of the taxable income generated by the business/company itself and then those that serve under it. In fact, we can go as far as to say that the businesses created by entrepreneurs create new wealth.

While existing businesses may not be able to surpass the glass ceiling created by the market in which they operate—which hinders how much taxable income they can generate—new businesses that offer better products and services allow for the creation of new markets that shatter conventional glass ceilings thus allowing for the creation of more wealth.

The other aspect of this is that when unemployment rates are high, it becomes difficult for the government to generate wealth because essentially, it has no people to tax (of people filling their income tax returns).

When entrepreneurs create new jobs, they increase the earning and spending power of those in their payroll, which as you can imagine, greatly benefits the economy because with more people earning 'good' money, the government does not have to struggle with tax collection.

3: The social change and communal development factor

Another great thing entrepreneurs do is bring about social change. This comes through the unique/novel goods and services they offer. Most entrepreneurs refuse to tie themselves to conventional ways of thinking and doing things, which is perhaps why the most successful entrepreneurs are those who buck tradition and create new products, services, and business systems that support the growth they want to see. The result of this is great social change.

Think back to the idea of electricity. If it did not exist in our lives, what kind of life would we be living? The invention of electricity by a great entrepreneur brought about many social changes to our lives and world.

Smartphones and smartphone apps are another great example of social change brought about by entrepreneurial thinking. When you consider smartphones (and apps) and the impact they have on society, you will agree that on top of making some entrepreneurs very successful and wealthy, they have also greatly changed how we work, play, and learn.

We cannot fail to mention that thanks to globalization, the social change brought on by innovative business thinkers is no longer local. Because of the internet and the systems it has created, it is easy for an app to have global social impact. For example, an App such as DuoLingo, an app that helps you learn a new language in the most convenient manner, is creating social change on a global level.

The other aspect of entrepreneurship is that it brings about community development in the following sense. Most successful entrepreneurs (and even not-so-successful entrepreneurs) go out of their way to offer mentorship to other entrepreneurs on a local and even international level. These businesses also dedicate a lot of time and money to the development of the communities in which they operate. For instance, in developing communities, companies and businesses that operate in those communities will help the community by building schools, roads, and other social amenities such as stadiums and the likes. Some even go as far as to offer financial support to local charities.

Take the example of Bill Gates. Through the Bill and Melinda Gates foundation, companies owned by Bill Gates have been able to offer financial support to great causes such as entrepreneurial development and public health. This has had great societal/community development.

The other thing worth noting and mentioning here is that existing businesses, especially those created by innovative entrepreneurs, are very central to how the government views and handles entrepreneurs and their businesses.

At the most basic level, when creating laws, rules, and regulations that govern how business operate, the government often consults the body tasked with private businesses lobbying. Governmental regulation is very central to the success of a private-business (from an entrepreneurial perspective) in that if the laws that govern the business are restrictive, it will undoubtedly affect growth and may lead to unwanted social outcomes such as an unfair market, corruption or worse, a financial crisis.

At this point in the guide, you should have a firm understanding of who an entrepreneur is, what it means to be one, how entrepreneurship differs from self-employment, as well as the kind of positive impact entrepreneurship has on society and the world at large.

Having discussed that, we'll now move to the next part of the guide where we will start discussing the essential knowledge you need to have to start a successful business venture not as a self-employed small business owner, but as a successful entrepreneur with growth and expansion in his or her mind.

Part 2: Business Systems and Environment

Businesses—especially successful ones created by innovative entrepreneurs—exist within a specific environment or space. For instance, apps exist within the larger IT ecosystem. For a business to achieve massive success, the environment within which it operates must be ideal for growth and expansion, otherwise the business, no matter how great and well set up it is, will suffocate and die.

In this section, we will talk about business systems and environment with the intention being to understand how the environment within which the business operates affects its success and profitability.

Chapter 6: About Business Systems

We can define a business system as the combination of the parts that form the business as a whole. This means a business system consists of the various factors that help an individual business achieve its objective.

Most business enterprises consist of several sub-systems whose balance and cordiality make up the business as whole and are central to its success. By applying a system approach to business operations, we can divide complex business systems into easier to manage components and activities—of each sub-system—so that in the end, we can define the roles of each subsystem and more importantly, the percentage of business success determined by that specific component.

For instance, we have the marketing system that handles all marketing endeavors; we have the finance system that handles all matters finance; the production system that handles the production of goods and services where applicable, the human resource system that is responsible for managing and ensuring proper utilization of the available human resource.

The main sub-systems in a business also have subsystems of their own. For instance, marketing can have a social media marketing system while production can have sub-systems such as machines, etc.

Basic Ingredients of a Business System

Since most business systems are unique in their own right, which is why they have sub-systems, how you set up your business system will largely depend on your objectives for that specific system.

With that said, most business systems have the following:

- Plans: The objectives the system intends to achieve as well as the methods by which it will achieve them.

- Inputs: The necessary input required to help the business actualize its plans irrespective of the available energy, information, or material.

- Process: The means used by the system—and its relevant subsystems—to convert the input into profitable output.

- Outputs

From this, we can represent a business system as follows:

Input

Input relates to the necessary resources 'injected' to support a business. It can consist of information, material, money, human and non-human resources, etc.

Process/Processing

This means the factors of production; it entails things such as production, information processing, personnel, marketing and the likes.

Output

This consists of the goods and services developed by the production/process and the compensation to employees, owners, business partners and associates, etc.

Other than the above, the business system also greatly depends on feedback in that if the output results are not ideal or acceptable to business partners and customers, it provides a way by which to adjust resources/input and the process for better efficiency and management.

For a business to thrive and succeed, all the parts that make up a business must work well and in coordination; this unification ensures the business system achieves its main objective whatever that may be.

This is where the entrepreneur comes in and creates management systems whose purpose is to ensure that the business system works appropriately and that the necessary resources and input go into the right places and areas where they will have the most impact on the overall success of the business.

Having talked about that, let us now talk about business environment, more specifically, how different environmental systems affect the operations and profitability of a business.

Chapter 7: About Business Environment

The environment in which a business operates greatly determines the success of any business enterprise since no business can operate in a vacuum. The environment influences business just as much as the business itself influences the environment.

An entrepreneur who fails to improve his/her relationship with the environment of the company is gradually leading the business to failure. Therefore, the level of interaction will also determine the level of success of the company.

How the Environment Affects a Business

A business and the environment in which it resides affect each other greatly. In fact, the relationship between a business and the environment (not the general environment of course) is what we can call a reciprocal relationship.

The environment provides inputs in the various forms discussed in the previous chapter, and then the business then provides the output in the form of goods and services. When the environment in which the business operates finds the goods ideal and useful, the interaction continues and the business thrives (so does the environment thanks to what we discussed in chapter 5). In cases where the output is not up to par and the environment does not accept it, the business changes its plans and business systems to meet the requirements of the environment.

Businesses and their environment interact on the following levels:

- The prevailing economic conditions within the environment in which the business operates influence the business. For instance, in the 2007 financial crisis, most businesses—especially those in the building and construction industry—reduced their production rate. On the other hand, seasons such as Christmas see businesses such as Amazon stockpile Christmas merchant in readiness for the impending business boom when the environment changes.

- Another instance of this relationship is when, for instance, other businesses such as banks and raw material providers, decide to change their rates. In the case of lenders such as banks changing their rates, the environment created can force a business to look for other forms of funding such as angel investors who are willing to fund the business for a stake. In this case, we see that the financial environment within which a business operates casts an influence.

- The workers, shareholders, and suppliers of a business, what we call the microenvironment, also affect the business and its operations just as much as the business affects them. The role of an entrepreneur is to ensure that even as workers demand a pay rise, suppliers demand better fees, and shareholders look for more dividends, the demands of the microenvironment do not negatively influence the business in any way. An amicable resolution of the above ensures overall satisfaction from all quarters, which positively affects the business and the environment. Failure to satisfy and reconcile these needs against business needs leaves the business at the mercy of the environment.

- The other interaction is on an informational level. Most businesses use the environment as an information cache. This information may revolve around buying trends, customer needs and wants, technological advancements in the field, competitors, ideal pricing, government policies, lending rates, and the likes. When the business receives this useful information, it has to measure them (their effect) against their objectives, goals, and financial obligations to its respective shareholders and partners.

- The most basic function of a business is to convert input into output. This only happens when the business in question has a very strong connection with its environment. The environment provides the input that the business takes and turns into output using productive facilities provided by the environment. The business then sends the output back into the environment for consideration. By receiving from the environment feedback about the output, the business can tweak the input and process to enhance its output and performance.

- The environment also presents the business with challenges (disguised opportunities) that it must overcome and exploit to turn profitable. Against the backdrop of the input provided by the environment, a business must go out of its way to minimize the impact of its weaknesses (and even turn them into strengths).

As you can see from this discussion, the business and the environment affect each other on many levels. The effectiveness and success of a business greatly depends on successful interaction between the business and its environment.

Below is a representation of how a business and the business environment affect each other:

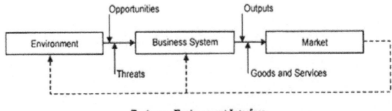

Business - Environment Interface

Environmental Factors that Influence a Business

Depending on the type of business in question, some environmental factors that can influence a business include:

1: Currency exchange rates

This relates to the value of the American dollar to other currencies. If the value of the dollar is high, it discourages importation of foreign goods and services. If it is low, it encourages business since it reduces the prices of imports.

2: Technological factors

Whenever you are about to start a business, ask yourself; does the environment have the necessary technology to use the product?

3: Socio-cultural factors

Social changes can come in the form of new dresses, new health and eating habits, new form of movement etc. These can pose either a threat or an opportunity to the business enterprise.

4: Growth rate

An increasing growth rate will be an advantage while a declining growth rate will be a disadvantage to the entrepreneur.

5: Demographic factors

We can define demographic factors as the various elements that businesses use to determine and create product offerings for their consumers. In essence, demographics are the elements/traits that businesses use to identify their main customers. For instance, a company may decide to group customers by age, location, earning power, and the likes. Segmenting consumers in this way makes it easier for the business to create effective marketing messages and material.

Some of the main factors that influence a business include income, which is one of the greatest factors that affects a business, its systems, and the business environment. The main things here is that a business must create goods and products that appeal to specific income groups. A great example of this is a case where a business creates high-end products for its high-income clients.

Age is yet another key demographic factor that affects business and its operational systems and environment. Likewise, businesses mainly create goods and services targeted at specific age demographics. For instance, tech companies often target younger people because this demographic is very tech savvy. On the other hand, baby boomers (those born between 1946-1964), of which the United States has 76 million of them, the largest population segment, are more attuned to services and products attuned to saving, investing, and vacationing. Age greatly influences which segment a business markets to as well as how it enters that market.

Geographical location is the other demographic factor worth considering. Here, it is important to note that buying options vary and change depending on geographical location. A great example of this is how some geographical locations prefer certain goods—foods and drink flavors are a perfect example— more than they do others. Enterprises that deliver the goods and services desired by specific locations stand to profit greatly.

6: Political and legal factors

You cannot create a business that deals in marijuana in an environment where marijuana is not legal. You cannot ask your customers to pay for your services using cryptocurrency in an environment where cryptocurrency transaction is unauthorized.

7: Competitors

This relates to understanding your competitors, their size, their shortcomings, etc. Sometimes it is better to start a different venture than trying to compete with some existing companies. Some companies have established themselves so well that it would take a lot effort and money to compete with them. Study your competitors very well and if you choose to compete with them, make sure your product addresses their shortcomings. In such a market, the products and services you offer should be a better that theirs.

As an entrepreneur, you must understand your environment and adapt accordingly. A great idea might fail because you implemented it in the wrong environment. You need to react positively to the environment and use the input it offers to create a great output that the environment accepts; that is the most absolute way to achieve entrepreneurial success.

As an entrepreneur, you need to ensure that the goods and services you offer are ones accepted by the environment in which you operate. You and the environment must have a reciprocal relationship in which each party is useful to the other.

Now that we have discussed the preliminaries of starting a business, we will now talk about how to start a business:

Part 3: Starting a Business

Starting a business is a very delicate process that you must pursue with a lot of care. The first step in starting a business venture is identifying a business opportunity. A business opportunity refers to a product or service needed by a particular demographic.

Usually, when starting a business, your hope is that your business idea will be an instant success. In most cases, however, that is rarely the case and things rarely turn out as expected. This is all understandable, as not all business ideas you will have translate to viable business opportunities.

For an idea to become a viable business opportunity, it must offer a viable solution to a problem experienced by potential consumers, a solution for which they are willing to pay to have.

Potential customers need to discover the value your business idea adds to their lives. In fact, now that you have decided to venture into entrepreneurship, your main responsibility is to discover ways of solving problems that your target market encounters at home, at work, at school etc. The solution to this problem can be a product or a service.

Because of the constant changes in the social, economic, political, technological and demographic structure of the society, we have tons of new business opportunities with new ones constantly generated in the economy.

You need to research and discover these business opportunities because they usually hide in the mud of confusion, failure, and other difficulties. The ability to decipher these opportunities is what distinguishes an entrepreneur from any other person.

With that said, you can improve your chances of spotting a business opportunity by closely examining areas that can help you generate useful ideas. Some of these areas are:

1: Copying existing business forms

This involves replicating a business structure with some modifications to distinguish the structure from other existing ones. These modifications could include making the product or service more convenient, less expensive, more performant, more durable, or even faster and easier to handle.

2: A Hobby

It is possible to transform a good hobby into a business enterprise. For instance, hobbies such as blogging, writing, traveling, cooking, reading, and speaking can become highly profitable businesses.

3: Vocation

Intelligent ideas can come from formal classroom or professional skills acquired. You can develop a ripe business opportunity in a classroom or in a conversation with a friend. Trade magazines, business newspaper, and journals can also provide business ideas that you can exploit. Moreover, managers and lenders of banks, venture capitalists and finance houses could provide intelligent business ideas that you can exploit.

4: Invention

As an entrepreneur, you are free to exploit new products and processes invented by an inventor. However, to do this, you must obtain, from the inventor, the license to exploit the patent rights.

If you do decide to follow this route, you will probably have to start your businesses from scratch, which presents challenges. However, the joy is usually great owing to the personal satisfaction you get from creating a unique enterprise.

Exercise

Pick a pen and a paper. Think about the problems around you (your society, community, country etc.) and write down potential business ideas that would solve these problems.

Now that you have that, let us flesh out some of the options you have as you consider which of the businesses to start:

Chapter 8: Buying an Existing Business (A How to Guide)

Now that you have your business idea (the ones you created from the thought exercise above), depending on the idea you have in mind, you have several options by which you can establish the business.

One of these options is a decision to buy an existing business and then perhaps improve upon it instead of creating a new business venture.

The Advantages of Buying an Existing Business

Buying an already established business has several advantages to it. Some of the most prominent ones include the following:

- An existing business has an existing and established customer base that you can easily exploit and improve.

- When you decide to buy an operational business, you bypass many of the operational problems involved in setting up a new business venture. When you buy an existing business, in most cases, all you need to do is improve the operational elements of the business.

- An existing business offers you a rare opportunity to exploit valuable strategic information concerning competitors, customers, suppliers, and the community at large, information provided by the business environment and that you can find from the company records or even from the previous owners.

- An existing business will also afford you trained and

experienced workers who are willing to remain in the business enterprise. Such workers can be especially important because they understand the processes and the systems that make up the business. Having such people on board will make the transition easier.

- When you purchase an old business, you also take advantage of the site, licenses, technology and other relationship enjoyed by previous owners.

The Disadvantages of Buying an Existing Business

Like most things, buying an existing business also has its fair share of disadvantages. The most standout of these disadvantages are as follows:

- In most instances, the actual reasons for the sale of the business may not be very visible for you to see. In some case, sellers of the business may keep from you specific information that prompted the need to sell—perhaps the owner wants to sell because the business enterprise is unprofitable. When you do decide to buy an existing business, you need to be very careful. You need to investigate the facts behind the decisions to sell.

- The business enterprise may be suffering from a bad reputation, bad contracts engaged by previous owners, or cases in court.

- It can sometimes be difficult to ascertain the true value of the company. As you decide whether to buy an existing business, consult a qualified accountant and other valuation experts who can help you ascertain the true value of a business.

- The organizational culture deeply entrenched within an existing business could also pose problems. The easiest way to overcome this is by bringing on board a new managerial style that suits your desired outcome and drives the business into profitability.

- Depending on which business idea you want to implement, going into business by buying an existing business is a sound decision. However, before you go all-out and buy the business, you need to consider several things that we will detail shortly. Before that, let us detail how to buy an existing business (the various steps you need to pay attention to):

How to Buy an Existing Business: The Steps

First, let us dispense a common myth. It is not true that just because a founder has decided to sell a business, there is something wrong with that business or that the business is about to crumble and fail. Yes, in some cases, the finances may be in a hole, but that is rarely the case.

In truth, various reasons can prompt the desire to sell a business. For instance, the founder may be transitioning and the business no longer fits his or her chosen lifestyle—for instance, if a founder/business owner has decided to take up global travel, it makes sense that he or she would want to sell.

No sane person would put a bad business up for sale. Most founders understand that before you decide to put pen to paper and actually buy their business, you will have done your due diligence. They, therefore, are likely to be very honest about why they have made the choice to sell the business. In most cases, the main reason is disconnection between lifestyle and passion for the business.

With that in mind, here are the steps you should take when buying an existing business:

Step 1: The Decision Phase

Because of the monetary and time commitment you will have to dedicate to a business—new, existing, or otherwise—before you buy a business, you need to think through the decision very carefully.

The first decision you have to make is to determine what you want, i.e. the kind of business you want to purchase. This is very important because the kind of business you decide to get into will undoubtedly become your life for a substantial amount of time.

In this regard, you should consider the following:

- The location of the business: We discussed how the physical environment in which a business operates in affects its input and output—we said that you cannot operate a marijuana business in a locality where growth, sale, and use of marijuana is not legal. The other consideration that relates to location is whether the business you intend to purchase is close to home. If it is not, it will prompt you to move. Are you ready for that? Locality will determine many things such as municipal licenses, labor cost, cost of inputs, taxes, and other elements that will have a very visible effect on the bottom line.

- The size of the business: Is your intention to own a business you can scale easily, such as a bustling enterprise, or a large business that has several branches across the country or do you prefer to take ownership of a small business? The size of the business matters because it will influence the output. Larger businesses will cost more (in terms of money and resources) but will have the advantage of offering bigger profits.

- The industry of operation: Ideally, you should only purchase businesses that are right up your alley, i.e. businesses that operate in an industry in which you are knowledgeable. For instance, choose to purchase businesses that align with your hobbies and passion so that you have enthusiasm and motivation for their pursuit.

These are the most dominant factors to consider when determining the kind of business you want. Later, we will have a checklist you can use to determine if the business you want to get into is ideal and ready for purchase.

Step 2: The Research Phase

Now that you have determined the kind of business you want to get into, the next part of the process is to research the kinds of businesses available in this field and available for sale.

At this point, avoid using Google to find businesses up for sale (unless of course your interest is a blog or online business in which case you can visit the various platforms like Shopify Exchange, Flippa and many others that sell domain and existing online businesses).

The first thing you should do however is look into your social circle to determine if a business you would want to own and purchase is up for such an offer. For instance, if your friend who started a macadamia processing plant is ready to travel the world as he has always wanted, that may be a business opportunity for you (assuming of course owning a business in that industry aligns with your hobbies and passions—this is very important).

On the other hand, if you know of a business you would die to own, you can approach the owner with the question; it never hurts to ask and you never know -perhaps the owner is ready to sell and go temple hoping in Thailand.

After failing to find a potential business within your social circle, you can then extend it to your business circle, the local community, and eventually the internet—being very careful with this one and only using reputable platform such as BizBuySell and other reputable platforms that offer online businesses for sale.

Step 3: The Business Broker Aspect

If putting out offers within your social circle and immediate community does not turn up favorable results, consider working with a business broker as a last choice. A business broker does the work of prescreening potential businesses for you. He or she can also make you aware of business enterprises that may interest you, and above all else, negotiate favorable sales terms when you do decide you are ready to buy a specific business.

Yes, a business broker can be a bit expensive. Most of them will charge you a commission of 5-10% of the sale price and except very few that will have a system where they charge you per hour of work done, most will only earn their fee once you make the decision to purchase a business. If you go the business broker way, be careful and avoid making hasty decisions about which broker to use or which business to buy. Do your due diligence.

Talking of due diligence...

Step 4: Do Your Due Diligence

After searching and finding a business that fits you, you will be very eager to make an offer. In fact, once you see the business and notice that it aligns with your goals, passions, and hobbies, improvement ideas will be popping into your mind as constantly as you breathe. Rein in the excitement because if you jump feet first without doing your due diligence, you may live to regret the decision.

Before you make an offer, research the business as a matter of necessity and prudence because even businesses that look great on the surface could be hiding many skeletons in their closets.

We will have a checklist of things to check shortly.

With that stated, the first thing you ought to do is avoid being the one making the offer or involving yourself too intimately in the process. Remember that now that you have determined a certain business is ideal and ripe for exploitation, the many improvement ideas going through your creative mind are likely to blind you to other things.

Because of this, create an adept acquisition team. The team can comprise of an attorney, a valuations expert or firm, a broker if you are using one, and any other person that will help you make a sound business decision after determining the state and health of the business.

Once you have an acquisition team ready, ask for a business variation report. This will reveal the worth of the business, which will help you determine if the business is worth the purchase especially considering the influence the business owner and his/her connections may have on the overall business value.

Ask your accountant to take a proper and detailed look at the financials of the business. This will make sure you do not buy a business that is in the hole financially or at the very least, if you do decide to buy a staggering business, know what you need to put in terms of effort and money to dig the business out of a financial hole and on the path to profitability.

Always remember that entrepreneurs are risk takers; it does not mean you should go in blind. Question everything that seems vague on the financial statement. Information is power here.

Due Diligence: Buying an Existing Business Checklist

As you do your due diligence, take specific notes of the following aspects of the business. They will help you determine the state of the business, which will help you tell whether it is worth your time and money:

1. **Inventory:** Take note of all the products and materials available in inventory. Ideally, your acquisition team should be there during an examination of the inventory. Knowing the inventory at hand well will help you greatly in

the negotiation stages.

2. **Fixtures, equipment, furniture, and buildings:** In general, these fall in the asset category. Ensure you have a full list of what the business owns, including the make and model number of each piece of equipment. This will help you with proper valuation and help you see what you have in hand before you get to work.

3. **Copies of legal documents and contracts:** Here, ask the current owner for all legal contracts he or she is in; this may include lease agreements, purchase agreements, contractor and sub-contractor agreements, sale contracts, and all other agreements that are legally binding to the business. You should also ask for other documents such as patents, articles of incorporation, trademark registration, and any other piece of document and contract that will help you make a sound business decision. Lease agreements are especially important to consider because in some cases, they are not transferable.

4. **Incorporation:** Ask the owner if the business is incorporated and check its operational mandate (state of registration and the likes).

5. **Tax returns:** Ideally, you should scrutinize tax returns for the past 5 years or more. This will give you an analytical view of whether the present business owner uses the business for his or her personal needs such as charging personal expenses to the business and the likes. Here, employ the services of CPA so you can get a clear view of the business's obligation to the federal government.

6. **Financial statement:** Likewise, you should ask for the

financial statements for the past 5 years or more. Once you have these statements, scrutinize them and have your accountant do the same, and then compare them to the filed tax returns. This comparison is especially important because it will help you determine the business's earning power. Looking at the financial statements will also help you compare the operation and sales ratio to those of the industry.

7. **Sales records:** Annual sales records will appear on the financial statements. However, it is prudent to check the monthly sales data and as you do, break the sales data by products and cash vs. credit sales. This will allow you invaluable insight into how the business is doing and the various cycles it goes through (and how they affect sales).

8. **List of liabilities:** Ask your acquisition team— specifically your attorney and accountant—to scrutinize the liabilities and come up with a proper valuation of cost and legal ramifications of the liabilities. Find out if the present business owner/s has (have) a loan commitments tied to any of the assets owned by the business and the likes. Ask about lawsuits and unrecorded liabilities such as out-of-court settlements, employee benefits, and the likes.

9. **A list of all accounts receivable:** Once you have the list of account receivables, segment it into 30, 60, or 90-days segments. The idea is to get a clear picture of receivables by age—longer outstanding periods lower the account value. From this segmentation, create a list of the top 10 accounts in order of their creditworthiness. For creditworthy clients whose account is outstanding beyond the 60 days mark, it may pay off to enforce a stricter credit

collection policy.

10. **A list of accounts payable:** Likewise, break the accounts payables into 30-day segments and use these segments to determine how much cash flows through the business. If the business has too many overdue account payables, determine if the creditor has placed a lien on any company asset.

11. **Debt disclosure:** Get a proper picture of all outstanding loans, notes, and any other debt accrued by the business including loans to customers.

12. **Merchandise returns:** Turn to the monthly or periodical sales data to determine the state of merchandise returns. If the rate is high, aim to identify why that is the case. This will help you determine how you can correct the trend.

13. **Consumer patterns:** You should be able to get a glimpse of this from the sales data available to you. Do not purchase a business that does not track customer purchase patterns (this will depend on the type of business of course). Taking a proper look at this data will give you a clear picture of the state of the business in relation to its customer base. It will also help you identify buying trends.

14. **The marketing plan:** Ask the owner about his or her marketing plan, how he or she acquires new customers, as well as how he or she maintains existing ones. For instance, does he or she advertise on social media or use offline advertisement strategies such as print and video media? Having an idea of the strategies used to market the business will give you a great view of how the environment

in which the business views the brand.

15. **Cost of advertising:** This should appear on the financial statement but it does not hurt to ask for separate records of the same. Analyzing advertising costs, especially when you compare the input versus the sales data, will allow you to determine if the business is getting a proper return on investment.

16. **Price checks:** Look at all the available products versus the available inventory and determine current price, discount price, and previous price increases. Benchmark these against industry standards and use the data to determine if you can comfortably increase the price of individual products.

17. **Industry standards and market history:** Once you have all the data you need from a business, properly scrutinize how the business fairs against industry and market standards. Pay special attention to how the sales in the market and industry are doing. A decline in market sales could be indicative of a shrinking market while a growing market and industry could be indicative of healthy competition.

18. **Location:** We talked about this at length earlier. Look at the location of the business and the area it markets to and determine how you can improve it. If a business has to incur great transport costs to transport its goods to retailers and input material to its production warehouse, moving the business premises closer to its retailers and suppliers may be in order to minimize expenses.

19. **Reputation:** This is in line with the marketing and

branding strategy. To determine how the local community views a business, you can check local listings or use the various review platforms on the internet. You do not want to buy a business that has a sullied image in the environment it operates within—branding is an asset in itself. Looking at things such as bank statement, merchandise returns, account payable and receivable, and various other streams of data will also help you determine the reputation of a business. Another nifty trick is to survey customers and interview workers.

20. **Seller-account relations:** Some businesses do business with close relatives for instance, with the customer/relative being a main buyer. If a business you intend to buy has such an arrangement—which you can determine from the financial records—determine how large a portion of the sales accounts for this and if the customer is willing to stay on after the sale goes through.

21. **Organizational chart and list of all employees:** This is especially important because key employees are often an asset to a business. Knowing who is in charge of whom and what will greatly help you determine where you need to make changes to influence growth since managerial practices greatly influence output. Having this information at hand will also help you see employee remuneration as well as any contracts the business may have with their unions.

22. **OSHA compliance:** If you are buying a business that creates products, it would do you well to determine the facilities in use meet occupational safety and health requirements and has passed all inspections. This helps

you ensure you are not buying a business the Occupational Safety and Health Administration (OSHA) considers unsafe.

23. Insurance: This is just as important if not more important as everything else we have discussed thus far. Determine if the business in question has an insurance coverage policy and the nature and type of the coverage policy. Determine the underwriter, the point person for the underwriter, as well as the insurance premiums paid.

If you check the 23 things above and still determine you are ready to purchase, continue to the fifth step below:

Step 5: The Funding Phase

Now that you have done your due diligence and perhaps determined that the business you want to purchase is actually in great shape, you can now start looking at financing options especially if the premise of buying is an expensive one.

If you do not have a private backer or are not independently wealthy, you will need to seek funding before you can purchase the business. Here, you are free to source your funds in whichever way you see feasible in the same way you would raise capital for a new business.

Some great financing options are:

- **Seller financing**: In this option, the owner allows you to stagger payments over time. In most cases, this type of deal is a bit expensive because it is a kind of hire-purchase plan and most owners will seek to have you pay the initial purchase amount plus interest. On other hand, it has its fair share of benefits one of them being staggered payments.

- **Partnering**: In this option, you can collaborate with a venture capitalist or angel investor whose interest in the business matches yours. Often times, the collaboration sees the investor act as the financier and you as the operations. The trade of—to the fact that you will not be investing a cent of your money—is that when the business proves successful, your profit margins will be lower.

- **Loan**: Loans are another great way to finance the purchase of a business (or even to finance the establishment of a new one). Long-term loans are especially great. However, taking a loan requires a great credit rating. Fortunately, you will not lack for a loan primarily because lenders are often eager to offer loans for the purchase of existing businesses that have a proven record.

How you choose to finance the purchase of the business is entirely up to you. Each financing option has its fair share of advantages and disadvantages. Choose one that is right for you and then move on from there.

Step 6: The Agreement Phase

Having done your due diligence and put together your financing, you are ready to purchase the business; all that remains now is to append your signature (and that of the former owner) to the sales agreement.

As stated earlier, engage the services of an able lawyer who combs through every clause of the sales agreement before you append your signature. A lawyer will help you understand the terms of the sale and everything else you need to be aware of before you actually purchase the business.

These are the basic steps detailing how to purchase an existing business. With that in mind, let us move on to the next chapter:

Chapter 9: Choosing a Business Opportunity—Evaluating Your Business Ideas

In some instance, you will get lucky and unearth several business opportunities from which to select. Determining which opportunities to exploit could be time-consuming and costly.

To make the process easier, use the following criteria to choose a business opportunity that is ripe for the picking.

1: Skills

Every business enterprise requires certain core skills. These skills may be purely technical such as the ability to manipulate and use certain equipment and tools or the ability to execute procedures and processes such as finance, marketing, legal or administrative processes etc. Always choose to venture into business enterprises that match your skillset or that you are excited enough about a business idea that you are willing to learn the necessary skills before getting into the business.

2: Experience

This refers to the deep and fundamental knowledge associated with that business. Acquisition of this knowledge usually comes from practice and being in the business/industry. Such experience provides you with the background knowledge of business practices in the industry such as purchasing, ethics, norms, customer service, particular ways of handling stakeholders, and even jargons associated with that line of business.

3: Personal Interest and Lifestyle

Your personal interest and lifestyle needs to fall in line with demands of the business. These demands include physical and mental effort, hours of work, work conditions, travel requirements, meeting people, solving problems etc. Most businesses fail because the owners are not prepared to meet the demands and challenges associated with the business and the business environment.

4: Support

The support from family members, friends, and associates is very important to the survival and success of a business. The opinion of people close to you now that you have decided to start a business is an important factor that can make or break the enterprise.

5: Capital

You need to have the ability to raise the capital needed for business and its individual projects and product development. This capital is necessary for the purchase of fixed assets, operating capital, material input, as well as what to put aside as operating balance.

6: Risk

The amount of risk involved in starting and running your business needs to be tolerable. As you probably already know, each business has a degree of risk unique to that specific business, industry, and market segment.

7: Regulatory constraints

There are some legal or regulatory guidelines provided by government in respect of some businesses such as pharmacy, clinics, and higher institutions. Before you dive head long into a business venture, ensure you can meet such requirements.

8: Income Level

The income generated from the business venture needs to be adequate for such basic requirements such as housing, clothing, food, recreation, entertainment etc.

Now that you have these criterions in mind, below is a systematic process by which you can test your business ideas to determine their suitability:

Testing Your Business Ideas: How to

If you have noted several needs in the market, needs you intend to fulfil or problems you intend to solve by creating a thriving business, you need to test out these ideas (the criterion above should help) before you decide which business enterprise you should venture into first (avoid launching into multiple markets at the same time. Slow and steady wins the race).

Take your ideas through the following process to determine which one has the most profit potential. Once you establish yourself in that market, you can then move to implementing your other business ideas:

Macro Testing

Macro testing is what you do before you start validating your business by testing the specifics of the business venture. Macro testing involves various things. The most affluent of these things include the following:

1. Asking (yourself and the environment) the right questions: The first rule of entrepreneurship is clarity of ideas and end goal (what we call the big picture). Going into business with half-baked ideas is a recipe for massive failure. To clarify your business idea or vision (for a new business or one you just bought), you need to ask yourself the right questions. The most logical thing to do is grab a pen and paper and consider every aspect of your big picture so that by so doing, you can streamline your thought process and get it on paper (we call this writing a business plan, something we will talk about in a later part). Ask yourself questions about your goals, the problem/s you intend to solve, your target market and how best to reach them, the resources you have at hand, and all other relevant questions.

2. Research the competition: Unless you are moving into a new market, a healthy amount of competition is indicative of a healthy market that can accommodate the goods and services you intend to offer. When researching the competition, aim to know the kinds of service and products they offer and their marketing, pricing, and branding strategies. This will allow you a rare chance to see what has worked and not worked for them, which will help you formulate a plan of your own. It will also help you carve out a unique preposition for your business.

3. Capital evaluation: In the last chapter, we talked about how, to buy a business, you need to streamline your funding and capital sources. The same applies here. The business idea you implement will largely depend on the amount of capital you have at hand. As we stated earlier, your capital sources are personal and will vary.

4. Market research: You should not get into a market you have not gone out of your way to research. By market research, we mean you should research your target audience and the business environment. Target market research is the best way to test and validate your business idea. You can use surveys and questionnaires to create a persona of your ideal target customer.

There are various ways to go about testing your business idea on a macro level. The easiest of these ways is to use Google and other search engines to search for keywords related to the business you want to start. For instance, if you intend to create a platform that offers advice on LPO financing, you can plug these keywords and other relevant ones into Google search or Google Trends or use the Google Keyword planner to determine how many people are inputting these keywords into their search boxes.

Another thing you can do is use your industry knowledge to access industry reports (you can also use Google for this) or market analysis reports. This will give you access to a ton of market data.

Still on competition research, consider your business idea and from there, zero in on one of your main competitors, a company that offers products/services similar to the ones you intend to offer.

Macro research is actually about determining the nature of the current market (in terms of market size, growth potential, competition, and sales volumes) so that you can determine your unique preposition and the best way to go about marketing your unique products and services in the most effective manner.

Micro Testing

Once you have a fair idea of the market and its state, the next part of the process is micro testing, which, coincidentally, involves sharing your idea with others with the intention being to see what they have to say about the business idea.

The most effective micro testing technique is research your target audience. You can do this through surveys or in-person questions. The Starbucks strategy is an especially effective micro testing strategy. Here, you simply go to a few Starbucks shops around you and share your idea with 20 or so people. Obviously, you want to be covert about the prospect.

Approach these 20 or more people by saying you are a researcher working on project X or Y and would like to ask them a few questions. After saying yes, ask them if they use product/service Z (a product/service related to the one you intend to offer), and if they do, when they use it, and what they like and dislike about the product/service. Asking such questions will give you invaluable customer insight. Once you determine the kind of consumer you are talking to, you can then share your business idea with the person and listen to the feedback you get.

If you know your target audience well—and their hang out spots—you can find them online on Facebook groups, Reddit, and various other forums. Interact with them in the most natural way possible even as you seek to validate your business idea.

Repeat the validation process with all your business ideas until you settle on a business idea that has the most potential, a business idea that you can implement with the resources available to you presently.

Talking about resources, because we live in a technologically empowered world, as you move forward with your chosen business idea, you should pay special attention to the technology you use.

To this end, let us talk about putting together the technology necessary for your startup:

Chapter 10: Technology Selection–How to Select the Appropriate Technology

As you go about setting up your business, it will be critical that you to choose the right technology for your enterprise. This may involve the purchase of computers, printers, or even a manufacturing plant.

Each line of business has a wide range of technologies available for you to choose from. This therefore means that before you settle on specific technologies to use, you need to gather as much information as possible on the suitability and the reliability of the making a decision.

How to Select the Appropriate Technology for your Startup

We are going to discuss a detailed process you can use to determine the type of technology ideal for your startup/business:

Step 1: Consider business needs

Before you go ahead and start buying technology for your business, you should conduct a technology audit. If you are dealing with an existing business that you just bought, you can take inventory of all the pieces of technology within the business currently. On the other hand, if you are dealing with a new enterprise that you want to establish from scratch, your best bet is to look at your business process and from that, postulate the kind of technology required by each aspect of the process.

For an existing business, look at the existing technology and ask yourself, "is this piece of technology serving its purpose well?" Categorize your existing pieces of technology into good, bad, or requires improvement. This will help you determine if you have outdated pieces of technology that need replacement.

For a new business, ask yourself a variant of the same question, "which piece/s of technology would serve this process well?" Consider the process in question succinctly and then consider which piece of technology would be the best fit for it. For instance, which pieces of technology are ideal for communication, finance, and the manufacturing process?

Step 2: Consider business growth

Often times, the pieces of technology you need to purchase are expensive to say the least (this is why you need to be mindful about purchasing your technological infrastructure).

To ace the process—whether you are dealing with a new or existing business—the best thing you can do is consider the expected growth of the business and then choose technology that grows with the business. To determine this, you can look around at other businesses in the same line and consider the kinds of technologies they are using.

For instance, if you are a startup in the app business, with the intention of being able to accommodate 10,000,000 daily app users, you can look at apps that have this kind of capabilities to determine the kind of technology their parent companies are using. This will allow you a rare opportunity to learn if the technology they are using has posed problems, if they have found fixes for the problem/s, and if, with a bit of ingenuity, you can find a better solution that eliminates the problem altogether.

Considering your business needs and growth in tandem will help you eliminate the possibility of, at least to some degree, buying pieces of technology that your business will outpace.

Take the example of something such as manufacturing organic juice packs. If you buy a processing plant that can only process a maximum of 1,000,000 juice packs per month but after 6 months, demand grows to 4,000,000 juice packs, your business will have outgrown that piece of technology faster than your finances can keep up, which means you will have to upgrade and sell or donate the previous piece of technology.

When you consider future business needs and growth, you can easily determine the kind of tech your business will need as it grows, and then buy those pieces of technology right now.

Step 3: Consider needs over all else

As an entrepreneur, you must hone your ability to differentiate business needs from wants, especially on the technology front. Whenever you are choosing technology for your business, think about what the business needs to operate functionally and grow as best as possible. This is important because when you consider how rapidly technology changes, if you choose to buy what the business desires instead of needs, you will be chasing your own tail trying to keep up with technology. You will also spend a lot of money trying to purchase every new piece of technology. To avoid this, consider the technology your business needs and only buy that—especially relate it to where you will use it within your business process and how it serves your projected growth.

Step 4: Always have a ready backup

Technology can be unreliable and prone to failure on many occasions. You must plan for this eventuality by creating a backup plan; this ensures that when your technology malfunctions, which it is likely to do, your business does not shut down for a substantial amount of time, which as you can imagine, can contribute to loss of business and revenue.

For instance, a business that relies greatly on technology can benefit from analyzing how a technological disruption can affect the business processes as well as its impact on the business in general (we call this a Business Impact Analysis). Taking this step ensures that you know how technological failures can affect your business and you can create a backup solution that is always ready in the unlikely event that the technology you have in place fails.

Step 5: Consider personnel

Operating most pieces of technology—especially those in manufacturing and the tech industry—requires specialized skills and knowledge. For instance, installing specific pieces of software and hardware, maintaining and upgrading them may require special skills.

Whenever you are buying pieces of technology, it pays to analyze the required skills to operate and maintain that piece of technology. Considering this will help you determine if someone in your team has the necessary skills or if you need to hire someone with specialized skills.

Considering the personnel required to operate the technology in question will also help you consider if operating the technology requires special training. Training—especially in the use of technology—is especially rife in the manufacturing industry where your staff may need training before they can start using some hardware safely.

Without training, no matter how up to date your technology is, your business process will suffer greatly. For this reason, when buying tech, consider the kind of training necessary for essential employees. Keeping this in mind will help streamline your business process and ensure that you get the best value for money out of your tech investment.

If you consider these five steps, you will not go wrong with your technology purchases.

Chapter 11: About Choosing a Business Location

Identifying an ideal site for a new business venture or factory can be a delicate and difficult task simply because several competing factors influence the location of a business/processing plant. In the final analysis, the decision taken is a compromise.

When selecting a business location, consider the following important factors:

1: Access

Do not overlook this important factor. Consider how accessible your business is to deliveries—incoming and outgoing—its market and target audience, as well as other services. For instance, if your business relies heavily on deliveries, you may want to consider accessibility to local transport corridors.

Accessibility to various services determines many other aspects such as rental prices. Locations closer to commercialized and high density zones are costly compared to out of town ones. On the other hand, while they are cheaper, out of town locations also limit accessibility and you should consider how that affects your business operations.

The other aspect to this is accessibility to target market. If your business relies heavily on foot traffic and walk in customers (coffee and juice shops, eateries, and the likes), the location of your business must be accessible to the target market. You should also not forget the employee aspect too; if the business is not accessible to employees, the commute will greatly affect their productivity and output. Location also affects talent pool, i.e. getting the right people situated within your business.

2: Security

As you choose between two or more locations, keep in mind the security of the business location because other than influencing the safety of your premise, security can also influence other factors such as insurance premiums and any other additional security measures necessary.

Because business decisions normally depend on informational input from the environment, if you choose to operate your business from a crime prone area, the insecurity within the area will influence many of your decisions.

Considering the security of an area before you decide to setup your business in it will help you determine how prone to risk your business is; just because you are an entrepreneur and taking risk is part of the quest does not mean the risks you take should not be measured. When you know the security of an area, you can put in place adequate security measures.

3: Competition

While not super important, you must also consider how close your business premise is to other competing businesses. Competition is not always bad. Sometimes, having competition around you can provide some of benefit such as ready talent, availability of raw materials, and other things such as accessibility to key installations.

When you establish the level of competition around you as well as the competitors operating within the same vicinity, it becomes easier to research the competition and use this research to choose the right location.

Too much competition within an area could be indicative of a saturated market or area, which probably means that you should look at other areas depending on the business you have in mind. Some businesses such as car dealerships actually want to be near each other as a way to offer customers more options and thus better deals.

Likewise, when choosing a location for your business, consider your unique offering and whether the competition is offering something similar or your offering will be novel. If the offering is unique, its best to pick a location that has a ready market for your offering because having to go out of your way to reach your target audience may prove very difficult and strenuous on your resources.

4: Rates

By rates, we mean the cost of rental, operating licenses, utility bills, taxes and the likes. Some areas offer better rates and are thus ideal for businesses in the startup phase. When choosing a business location, it pays to consider the business rates levied by the locality/municipality/state within which your intended premise resides.

It may also be necessary to consider other rates such as rent deposit rates, parking rates, cost of goods and living as well as other rates that may affect your business overall. Such costs can greatly influence your location decision as well as other facets of your business operations.

Also, take into account minimum wage rates. These are very

important because other than influencing your balance sheet at the end of the month, wage rates will also determine the kind of skill you can attract to your business (in terms of employees and their skills). If your business is very technical and therefore greatly reliant on skilled workers, you will want to choose a location that on top of offering great talent, also offers pocket-friendly pay rates so that you do not break bank trying to outbid other enterprises for the little talent available.

Always remember that your employees are your greatest resource and therefore, you should balance between remunerating them well and ensuring that their rates are within reason and not too extravagant.

Remember that like a home, a business must run within a specific budget frame. Rates influence the budget and are therefore important.

5: Growth

As you consider your business premises, consider your future growth and ask yourself, "will this premise handle the expected growth?" This is important because once you establish your base of operations, keep in mind that moving to other locations to keep up with growth will be costly affairs in terms of time and money.

As you choose a location, consider whether the premises will serve for a short-term as you seek something more permanent or whether you want something permanent from the start. If you are shooting for the latter, it is best to consider future growth and the flexibility of the premise to accommodate that growth.

Ideal business locations will vary from business to business depending on their nature. To this end, choose a business location that fits your specific needs and enhances your business operations because this is what matters most. If you consider the 5 factors above, you will get it right.

Part 4: Product Planning and Pricing

The fundamental idea of product planning is the development of augmented products that are popular to every customer. There are two types of products:

1: Generic Products

These are original products or services offered to a target market.

2: Augmented Products

Augmented products are generic products or services upon which you, the entrepreneur, add solicited and unsolicited extras to attract the customer. These extras are normally in the form of added value; for instance, if you run an ice cream business, you can package the ice cream in a non-drip package that ensures the customer does not get ice cream all over his hands and cloths. This package is then a solicited package particularly when it is editable. This same extra can be a plastic cup that the customer can use to drink water later and because it is an unsolicited extra, it attracts the customer.

Whether solicited or unsolicited, these extras aim to produce cognitive consonance on the customer. Cognitive consonance is the positive post-purchase feeling that a customer experiences after buying a good or service. This positive post purchase feeling is surely personal satisfaction. On the other hand, cognitive dissonance describes the negative post purchase feeling that an individual has after buying a product or service. This is certainly a feeling of dissatisfaction.

While cognitive consonance can lead to repeat purchase,

cognitive dissonance may lead to customer rejection of the product in the future. As a good entrepreneur, you should strive to generate repeat purchases by creating cognitive consonance, which we have described as a feeling of total satisfaction with the product or service offered.

Product planning entails the deliberate activities you take to meet the demands of the customer when creating a product or service while taking into consideration the constraints of resources, government regulations, and the environment. It also includes decisions concerning the product range and the product line to engage in.

A **product range** refers to all the different types of products your business enterprise offers for sale. It refers to all the types of products your business places on the market for customer appreciation. A **product line** refers to a group of products closely related to each other. Different product items such as sweet drinks, lager beers, wines etc. are closely related to each other. A **product item** refers to a specific version of a product line.

The principal ambition of all product planning is fulfilment of customer needs. Product decisions involve two principal activities: to modify an existing product or to introduce a completely new product to the market. In both cases, the process is the same. Our focus today will be the development of a new product.

Before developing a new product, you need to make major decisions in two major areas. Firstly, you need to decide whether there is real need for the product or service in the market and secondly, determine the needed product or service. What product or service do the people in that particular environment need? For instance, what do you think are the particular products or services needed around your university campus?

Perhaps it is important to note that the failure rate of entirely new products in the market is relatively high. Moreover, the cost of developing and launching a new product is usually high. It is therefore important that you reflect deeply before engaging in the creation of a new product.

With that said, let us look at the process by which you can create new products:

Chapter 12: Steps in the Development of a New Product

The steps below are the most central ones to the development of a new product. These steps are not a scientifically proven procedure. Instead, use these steps as guidelines that can help channel your energy and resources as you seek to achieve entrepreneurial success. The steps are as follows:

Step 1: Idea generation

The first step is the need to generate ideas. These ideas can come from research work, brainstorming sessions with colleagues and other workers, salespersons, customers, production managers etc. Please brainstorm with your colleagues to come up with some business ideas either in class or at home.

In chapter 9, we talked about how you should go about creating a list of business ideas and then evaluate the profitability of each. When generating ideas, keep your mind on scalable ideas that are also relatively easy to implement with the resources you have at hand.

Step 2: Screening

Screening is the preliminary evaluation stage involving the systematic elimination of ideas that lack technical feasibility and ideas that are not consistent with the company's policies, philosophy, or product lines.

Develop specific criteria with which to determine if an idea should make it to the next phase of the process and then subject all ideas to the set criteria. One of the key criteria that should form part of your screening process is how the idea compares to the top three innovations in the market.

Step 3: Profitability Analysis

This involves the analysis of cost and the sales potential of the new product you intend to develop. Sales volumes normally depend on the price charged per unit of product. This involves many considerations such as operations up to market analysis and the potential market share.

Step 4: Production of Samples

These are the initial samples that may not necessarily go to the market. These are prototypes of the product; their role is to indicate the salient features of the future product. These initial samples also confirm cost estimates, with regard to operations, cost of raw materials, storage etc.

Step 5: Product Testing

In this phase, you distribute a good sample/prototype of the product to some chosen consumers/focus group, experts, and other concerned parties for evaluation. You then carefully collect their opinions and input, analyze it, and then use the results of the analysis to make a decision about the future of the product.

Step 6: Improved Product Development

This phase involves the manufacturing of the improved product based on the observations of the panel of consumers, experts, and concerned parties involved in step 5.

Step 7: Test Marketing

In step seven, you sell the improved product to a representative sample of the target market to determine its suitability. This process also gives you a rare chance to assess the pricing policy, distribution channels, and promotion plan. This sample market may also show you how the broader market will respond to the product. This will further provide concrete information as to whether to continue with the product or not.

Step 8: Actual launch

Once you decide to continue with the production of the product, the next step is to plan the product launch. At this stage, you need to choose a special date within which you will introduce the improved product to the target market and the public in general. You may also choose to introduce the product to the whole market or to introduce it gradually in a small geographical area and gradually expand to the whole market.

As part of the launch phase, you will have to think about how to package the product. The next chapter talks about this:

Chapter 13: About Product Packaging

We have already discussed generic products and the extras added to make it an augmented product. Packaging is one of the extras that you and your production team can add to make the product an augmented product.

Functions of Product Packaging

Packaging performs the following functions in product development:

1: Protection and Preservation

The first and important function of packaging is protection and preservation. We are talking about protection from physical damage and preservation from any form of contamination of the product when it is in transit, in the store, or even during usage.

2: Identity

Packaging may also indicate the identity of the product and information concerning its method of usage.

3: Promotion

Packaging can also come in handy for promotional activities through enhancing the beauty and aesthetic appeal of the product.

4: Convenient Usage

Packaging can also facilitate the convenient usage of the product e.g. think of ice cream packages.

Important Product Packaging Factors to Consider

Below are the most important factors to consider when choosing packaging for your products:

1: Functionality and quality

As we have stated, the main function of any packing is to ensure the safety of the product while in transit. Irrespective of the attractiveness and innovativeness of your choice of packaging, it must be functional and of superior quality depending on the product in question.

To this end, as you choose product packaging, go for high-quality material that ensures product safety as it travels from your production line, to the distribution centers, and onwards to the end consumer. In some cases, ensuring this may mean forking out more on quality product packaging with the advantage being that by choosing an ideal packaging material, you will minimize damage of goods in transit.

2: Design

The design of the packaging material will largely depend on factors such as the size and shape of the product in question. If possible, use standard packaging material because it improves convenience and flexibility throughout the product's lifecycle, i.e. storage, handling, and transport.

Additionally, by going the standard material route, you also reduce packaging cost (bespoke designs cost more). On the same note, however, just because you should go the standard packaging route does not mean you cannot enhance the visual aspects using intuitive branding and colors.

3: The Price

How cost-effective your preferred packing material is will greatly determine the price at which you sell the product. To this end, consider how much it will cost to package individual products and whether the material you intend to use offers the best cost-benefit. Ideally, you should use material that, on top of securing the product, also helps you save money. For instance, if you are not dealing with a brittle or easily breakable product, you can opt for lighter packaging material.

4: Storage and distribution

How long does a product stay in your warehouse before it moves forward through the distribution channel? Answering this question will help you determine the kind of packaging material you should use. Understanding the distribution channel should also help you understand how products move from you to distributors, to retailers, and then to consumers, which will help you determine how to package the product in a way that ensures that the customer gets the product in a pristine condition.

If your products have to travel a long distance, you are better off going with durable packaging material especially keeping in mind the mode of transport used to get the products to their end destination.

Always remember that the aim is to ensure that the product remains undamaged throughout the distribution process.

5: Compliance

The packaging material you choose should offer you long-term sustainability in that it should comply with industry standards and regulations. A good example of this is food packaging. If you are in this field, your packaging material should comply with all regulations and offer you long-term sustainability, i.e. you should be able to use the material long-term. For instance, you can use recyclable material.

Always keep in mind that packaging is very central to branding. If you ace product packaging and use the most adept and ideal material for your products, you will be a step closer to creating a lasting brand identity, which as you know, can greatly influence the success of your product and business in general.

Since we are talking about branding, let us flesh it out:

Chapter 14: Product Branding

Branding is a deliberate attempt to distinguish your product or service from those of the competitors; it (branding) involves every activity performed to distinguish the product from that of the competitors. These activities include the product or service name, the trademark, distinctive outlook and colors.

The **brand name** is the particular identity most used to identify the product or service from others. Great names of brand names include Sony, Apple, Samsung, Toyota, or Amazon. A brand name needs to be easy to pronounce and to remember since different and displeasing names are not easy to remember.

A trademark is usually a sign or symbol used to identify the product, service, or even the company. It may not necessarily be pronounced. These brand names and trademarks are usually unique to facilitate legal recognition and registration since once registered, no other company or business can imitate them.

Advantages of Branding

Product or service branding has the following advantages:

- It helps advertise the product/service through distinguishing it from others. Billboards, announcements, and other forms of advertisement will easily use the brand name to distinguish it from other products.

- Branding also facilitates the mass distribution of the product or service, which is very necessary for mass production. Branding allows for the quick identification and transportation of products to different distributors and consumers.

- Branding also facilitates competition, which brings with it better products, prices and facilities.

- Branding allows customers to identify the product easily thus preventing retailers from replacing them with fake and inferior products.

- Branding also gives the company its status and distinctive outlook.

You now understand the role of branding as well as what it means to the success of your products.

The Golden Rules of Product Branding

When it comes to acing branding (for your products and products packaging), keep the following rules in mind.

Rule 1: Keep it memorable

This is especially in relation to the name of the product/brand. Keep it memorable and avoid using generic brand/product names. If you look at the most memorable products and brand names, brand names such as Samsung, Apple, eBay, Google, PayPal, and the many other brands you can imagine, you will note that they have a memorable name, which in most cases, is a proper noun of something similar.

If you give your product/brand a generic name, it will be easy to forget and the possibilities of the product flying off the shelves will diminish greatly as your marketing train runs out of steam on which to run. While a generic name is not the only factor that can lead to the failure of a product or business, it also contributes because remaining in the minds of consumers, which is what great branding does, enhances your marketing strategies.

Rule 2: Keep it simple and clear

Always be clear—on the packaging—about the product name, the brand/company responsible for creating the product, and more importantly, what the product does because it takes consumers less than 4 seconds to look at a product, determine what the product is for, the brand behind it, and if the product is one the customer needs and should buy.

By keeping the packaging simple and clear, you give potential consumers all the information they need to have to determine if the product is for them. Keeping the branding on the packaging simple and clear also eliminates confusion for the customer.

Rule 3: Authenticity and honesty

It is very tempting to use your product packaging to depict your product as perfect. Do not try to hoodwink your consumers; they know better. For instance, if the product is question does not have fruit content (in the case of foods or juices), do not use pictures of fruits or the likes.

When you go out of your way to present a product in the best way possible, you ultimately deceive your consumers, the result of which will be disappointment in the mind of the consumer, something you do not want to happen because it will have an adverse effect on your sales and create a negative brand image.

Be honest with your product packaging. Keep it simple and make sure it clearly describes—in image and print—the product as it exactly is. Keep in mind that above all else, consumers want the expectations created by the product packaging to match their reality when they do finally unwrap the product. Yes, they expect you to embellish the packaging a little, but they do not expect a great mismatch between the packaging and the actual product. Be honest.

In terms of authenticity, make sure your packaging is also original and memorable. Keep in mind that your product will be competing with other products from other enterprises as great as your enterprise and run by perceptive entrepreneurs too. Authenticity is the only way to ensure your product/s stands out from the competition.

By authentic, we mean your packaging branding should be unique and creatively designed. Choose a look that appeals to your target audience (focus groups and surveys can help you with this) and avoid gong the generic route.

Rule 4: Shelf Impact

When you head to your local store/supermarket, you do not see products alone. You see them as veritable patterns thanks to the row and column-like arrangement and the distance from the shelves. This is to mean instead of seeing products in detail, all we see are the patterns made by the products as they rest on their shelves. This also means that the products that stand out are the ones that attract our attention. This is what we refer to as shelf impact.

Once the product is in a row or column surrounded by various other products, the distinctiveness of your packaging, i.e. how much it stands out, will greatly influence your sales. Ideally, you want your products to stand out as much as possible and therefore, when thinking about branding, you should think about how to make your product pop. The best way to do this is to simulate the placement (on a store shelf—several rows work best) within your business to determine if the look you have chosen is distinctive enough.

Rule 5: Practical

Did you know that Heinz greatly improved sales on their Ketchup product by changing the design of the bootleg (they inverted it, i.e. they turned it upside down)?

What Heinz did is change the practicality of their product packaging. Practicality relates to the actual size, shape, and functionality of the product as well as the labeling and wrap. By using a practical packaging design, you can also improve sales largely.

Packaging design/branding is a trial and error process that requires patience and lots of iteration. As you go through this process, keep the five rules above in mind and do not forget to follow your intuition because in the end, you know best the message you want your products and business to communicate.

Chapter 15: Product/Service Life Cycle

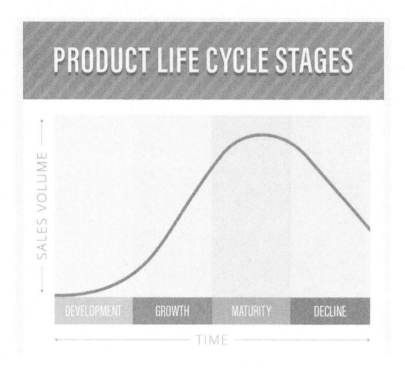

Like all living organisms, every product has a life cycle that begins with embryonic or introductory phase. At this stage, the product experiences steady rise in the volume of sales, which passes through the growth stage and reaches the peak at the saturation stage. The volume of sales starts dropping at the decline stage and it can finally die off if the company does not add other solicited and unsolicited extras to make it an augmented product.

At the maturity stage, competitive pressure increases as the popularity of the product is at is zenith. The profit margin starts reducing paving the way to the decline following changes in customer taste and other technical advances leading to product substitution. Price, promotion, and more effective distribution channels could effectively prolong the life cycle in the short term instead of creating a new product. Finally, in the end, product innovation becomes the only solution.

To help you understand this better, especially how the life cycle affects various aspects, including product pricing, let us look at each of the stages:

The Product Life Cycle and Its Effect on Your Pricing Strategy

First, a product's life cycle is a model used to symbolize how a product moves through its life cycle, from creation to discontinuation. The cycle has four stages namely *development*, *growth*, *maturity*, and *decline*.

By understanding this life cycle, you will be able to put in place a proper pricing strategy that will help you determine and manage sales and compete effectively within your target market.

The aim of tracking the product life cycle, a process called product life cycle management, is to ensure that as a product goes through the cycle, you can manage it and keep profits high (and losses at bay).

Understanding how to handle a product as it navigates through the life cycle also helps you know how to handle it in terms of pricing the product.

Here are the stages in detail:

Stage 1: Development

Development is the initial phase. It involves the introduction of the product to the target market. In this stage, since the product is new to the market, sales are low. If the product is novel and unique, sales will be lower.

During this stage, your best bet is to concentrate on potent marketing strategies that make your target audience aware of the product. Social media is an especially potent marketing strategy at this point.

In the development stage, your pricing strategy will greatly depend on your financial projections; you can price it low or high. If you go the low route, the product will penetrate the market faster and create a loyal fan base. Going the high route is also effective especially if you have established a ready demand for the product.

Stage 2: Growth

In the growth stage, the product experiences high demand and improved sales. This stage is especially great because your product is not a mainstay in the market. The drawback is that because the product will be gaining popularity, competitors will also be looking to usurp the product's dominance by creating similar or better products.

At this stage, you may also need to dedicate more time and resources to marketing in a bid to ensure that potential customers choose your product over others. It may also be necessary to lower your prices to make them more competitive.

Stage 3: Maturity

In the maturity stage, sales stagnate (stagnated sales growth) primarily because at this stage, most of your target audiences have or use the product; this reduces the demand, which means unlike the growth stage, your sales will not rise or increase.

When a product reaches this stage, most businesses choose to add another product line to the market as a way to keep up with the competition. At this stage, the best marketing strategies are ones that emphasis what is unique about the product.

When a product gets into this stage, you will have to adopt a competitive pricing strategy since the competition within the market will be fierce; aim to keep your prices low but not too low. You can also implement a discount pricing strategy.

Stage 4: Decline

Being the final stage in the cycle, the product sees less market demand. At this stage, you must decide whether to continue or discontinue producing and selling the product. If you choose to continue the product, you will have to look for ways to make it more competitive in the market.

In most cases, the decline phase comes about when competitors produce better or more novel products that get more attention, consumers lose interest in your product, or the product sales decline to a point where keeping it in the production line is no longer profitable.

In this stage, your best pricing strategy is to lower your product price to its breakeven point. You can also implement a discount pricing strategy to drum up more sales and purge backlog inventory. You can also try bundling where you bundle the product with another related product and offer both as discounted products.

The product life cycle is inevitable. The only thing you can do about it is to prepare how you will handle the product in each of the stages by deciding how you will price the product and keep it competitive once it enters a phase.

Chapter 16: Product Pricing

Pricing your products at the right price is an intricate process that requires careful thought and experimentation because if you price them too low, you may see improved sales but risk making the product appear as if of low quality. On the other hand, if you price your products too high, you risk reduced sales since the product may appear luxurious and thus only able to attract a well-off clientele.

Even before your product moves through the life cycle, you have to pay special attention to your pricing strategy because it will determine how you price the product all through the stages.

The main aim of a pricing strategy is to ensure that your product helps you generate sales and therefore profits and penetrates the market where it gains a foothold. The important thing to note here is that while profit is the main motivator behind product generation, not all products will be profitable, and in most cases, even unprofitable products can contribute to overall business profits. In such cases, the profits from the products enunciated by the loss-generating product are enough to keep the business operationally profitable. We call such a product a loss leader.

In product pricing, we have something called market skimming, a strategy where you decide to charge the best possible price for a product in the present moment with the intent being to generate as much profit as possible presently as the product navigates through the product life cycle and sales decline as customer needs change. This strategy is a sort of price discrimination using time.

Price discrimination using space comes when you decide to charge different prices in different, completely separated market segments to the extent that goods bought from the cheaper market segment become unsellable in the more expensive market segment.

In most cases, entrepreneurs set a product price that is sufficient for him/her just to earn the satisfactory amount of money called the satisfactory rate of return, irrespective of the possibilities to charge higher prices to earn more.

Whatever your pricing objective may be, you need to take into account fundamental considerations when determining the price of a product. These considerations are **cost**, **profit**, **competition,** and **demand** for the product.

In the end, the decision is about choosing whether you want to price your products higher and generate reduced sales volume, or price it lower and generate more sales but creating a compromised perception of the products quality.

The Most Effective Product Pricing Strategies

With this in mind, we have several pricing strategies you can use to price your products just right. The most popular ones of these include **Cost plus**, **Mark up**, **Going rate**, and **Binding**.

The simplest pricing strategy is what we call keystone pricing. The formula is relatively simple: you simply double the cost of the product to get a 50% markup. The mark-up, however can change up or down depending on the product in question and the specific situation.

The formula for keystone pricing, a formula you can use to

calculate your retail prices is as follows:

Retail price = [(cost of product) ÷ (100 − markup %)] x 100

To make this even easier, let us look at an example:

Assume the product you intend to price cost you $20 at a 45% markup; here is how you would calculate the retail price:

Retail price = [(20.00) ÷ (100 − 45)] x 100

The results of this are

Retail price = [(20.00 ÷ 55)] x 100 = $36

This simple formula is the most effective way to markup your products. Now that you know this formula, what follows are other product pricing strategies that will help you generate profits all through a product's life cycle and stay a step ahead of the competition all through the cycle:

1: MSRP (Manufacturer's Suggested Retail Price)

In this pricing method, a method common with retailers and ecommerce stores, your manufacturer sets the MSRP and you then use this to price your product using the keystone method but drop 1-5 cents of the retail price ($1.99, $9.99, etc.) with the intent of dropping the cent to implement psychological pricing.

This pricing strategy is very effective. However, because your manufacturer will be the one setting the prices and all you have to do is add the markup, you will have to find ways to differentiate yourself from competitors who also offer the same prices.

2: Psychological pricing

Research conducted to determine how shoppers feel when parting with their money revealed that costumers experience psychological pain—pain of loss when parting with money. Psychological pricing limits the amount of pain experienced.

As described above, in psychological pricing, you markup the price but reduce it by 1-5 cents such that a product you would sell at $10 sells at $9.5 or even $9.99. This strategy eliminates the mental barrier involved with purchases.

Further research has shown that by using this strategy and ensuring that your retail prices end in odd numbers, they will outsell other products whose price ends in even numbers.

3: Discount pricing

In this pricing strategy, you choose to sell goods under their normal retail price and under the prices offered by competitors. In most cases, this pricing strategy works best with volume-driven businesses that purchase large volumes of a product.

In the conventional sense of the word, sales, seasonal special, coupons, and markdowns are all perfect examples of discount pricing on a retail level. You should be very mindful with how you use this strategy because if not well implemented, the strategy can diminish profit margins to the point of losses.

4: Loss-leader pricing

We briefly talked about this earlier. We said that loss leaders are products that do not generate profits (or generate very little profit). Their main intent is to attract consumers to a deal in the hope that the said customer will buy a more profitable product or item. Black Friday and Cyber Monday are great examples of this strategy in play.

5: Cost-plus pricing

In this pricing strategy, all you do is add a markup to your total product cost including cost of material, manufacturing, shipping, and all other expenses.

These are the most effective pricing strategies/techniques. You can implement one at a time or any of them together.

Part 5: Preparing a Business Plan

Chapter 17: How to Create a Business Plan for your Business

A business plan is a roadmap detailing how to implement your business idea and what to do to get the business to where you want to see it. The main aim of a business plan is to help you organize your thoughts concerning the business and concretize your business goals.

Drawing a business plan is a very important exercise because it clearly describes why, how, and when you will start experiencing economic viability as you implement the business. A business plan clearly states when you think the business will start having a self-sustaining cash flow or economic viability. The "why" part of the business plan explains why somebody out of the organization should be interested in the product or service, which clarifies why somebody outside the company should be interested in and qualified to buy the product or service.

The "how" part exposes the human, infrastructural, financial, and other temporal resources needed to produce the good or service. When creating your business plan, you need a good balance or a mix of these resources to produce the good or service at the cheapest possible price.

The "when" aspect of the business plan enumerates the series of events that follow the plan and the timeline you intend to use to accomplish each event or milestone; it also presents the financial implications of each event.

The Rules

Like most things business-related, writing a business plan has some very specific rules you should follow. Here they are:

Rule 1: Short and precise

A business plan is not a memoir: keep it short and to the point as much as possible because the aim is to have people read it. If your business plan is too long, no one is going to read it. The other thing is that your business plan is a roadmap. That being the case, you will refer to it many times and you will need to refine it just as many times. When your business plan is long, this process becomes much more difficult.

Rule 2: Understand your audience

Since a business plan details how you intend to actualize your idea, its most central element should be a proper understanding of your target audience. In fact, most professionals suggest that, as you create the business plan, you use the language used by your target audience.

For instance, if you are writing the business plan with the intention of seeking funding from investors, write it in a language understandable to potential investors. This ensures that you keep the business plan short and that the plan is understandable.

Rule 3: Learn as you go

Creating a business plan is an especially intimidating undertaking for most entrepreneurs. It does not have to be. In fact, you do not have to be a business expert to create one. All you need is to understand your business well and then learn everything else as needed. You can start with a single page business plan (the lean plan) and then build it out as your vision clarifies with time.

Now that you know the rules, let us talk about the elements that make up a business plan:

The Essential Elements of a Business Plan

Usually, a good business plan should start with an executive summary. In reality though, you write the executive summary last. A good business plan has the following elements:

1. Executive summary

2. Opportunity

3. Execution

4. Organization and people

5. Financial plan

6. Appendix

We will now discuss each of these elements:

1: Executive summary

As implied earlier, while the executive summary takes up the first page of your business plan, you actually write it last.

The overall role of an executive summary is to introduce your business and explain what the business does; it also serves the purpose of explaining what you want the target audience, for example an investor, to do.

To ensure your business plan stands out, you need to create an adept executive summary that covers all the key highlights and that can act as a standalone document—most investors look at the executive summary to determine if a business is worth investing in.

Among the things you should do to ensure that your executive summary is in great shape include:

1. The top of the page should have a sentence (one sentence) that sums up everything your business stands for and intends to do or is doing. We also call this sentence your value proposition.

2. After the value proposition comes the problem. Here, you use one or two sentences to describe the problem solved by the business.

3. You then present the solution, which can be a product or service, and then very succinctly describe how the product/service solves the problem.

4. After stating the problem, you have to create a very short write-up of the person target by the solution you are offering. Go out of your way to state the nature of your target audience as well as how many of them exist because targeting is from where your marketing plan springs.

5. After this, define the competition because in most cases, the market has alternatives that your targets are currently using. Provide an overview of the competition.

6. Create a summary of the people within the organization (the team), who they are, and how adept they are at actualizing the business idea (you can list key skills of people in key positions).

7. A summary of your financial plan because it shows your projected sales and expenses, and by when you intend to

have achieved profitability. You can also use this space to explain your business model.

8. If the intention of the business plan is to solicit funding, succinctly describe what you need without going too much into detail (the details will come later). Simply state the amount of money you need to raise to fund your business idea.

9. Milestones and tractions make up the last element of the executive summary. These two describe the progress made thus far and the progress expected in the future.

If you do not intend to solicit funding, you can skip writing the executive summary (especially if the business plan is just a strategic guide for your business). Keep the executive summary one or two pages at most.

2: Opportunity

The opportunity part of the business plan is perhaps the most detailed part of the document. Here, you describe, in detail, the problem you intend to solve, the solution you are presenting, how your product or service solves the problem, as well as how it fits into the market within which it will compete. This is also a great chance to demonstrate what makes the solution unique and different from others in the market.

This part of the business plan covers the many things your executive summary fails to cover. It covers:

1. The problem and the solution: This is the first chapter of the opportunity section of your business plan. Here, start by describing the problem, the primary pain points, as well as

how target audiences are presently solving the problem. Pinpointing the problem and being able to explain it is the first step to validating a business concept. After defining the problem, define the solution you are offering as well as why it is the best solution for the problem. Describe what the solution is, how you intend to offer it, and to some degree, how potential targets will interact with the solution.

2. Target market: After detailing the problem and the solution, detail whom the solution targets, the people whose problem you will solve. This is a great opportunity to show how well you know your target audience and their needs, how many of the targets exist, and their various segmentation.

3. Key customers: Including this section normally applies to enterprise businesses that have not established their customer base. You can use this part of the business plan to provide details about your key customers especially if you sell to other businesses or have a few key customers that are integral to the success of the enterprise. Remember to detail their importance to the business.

4. Competition: After writing about your key customers, describe your competitors at great length. Who are they? What kind of solutions are they offering? How is the market reacting to their offering? How does the solution they offer compare to the one you offer? Which advantages do you and your product have over them and theirs? Using a competitor matrix is the best way to communicate this information. Importantly, make sure that even as you list down the competing solutions offered in the market, you

go out of your way to show how unique and different your solution truly is and how that difference will make all the difference to potential targets. We call this highlighting your advantages, something all investors will want to look at. Under no circumstance should you make the mistake of stating how you have no competitors.

5. Vision: Use this part of the document to highlight where you intend to steer the business in the future, the products and services you intend to offer in the future. Make this section brief; simply include a paragraph or two that shows your direction in regards to the business and its potential in the future.

3: Execution

After describing the opportunity (the opportunity is the solution you intend to offer the market), the next section is the execution part where you describe how you intend to execute the business. This part is also very important because it covers key areas such as how you intend to market the solution, drum up sales, how the business will operate, how to track your success, and the milestones with which you will measure the success (and by when you expect to have achieved these milestones).

The following are the key areas that make up the execution section of a business plan:

Sales and marketing

As the name suggests, this section of the business plan illustrates the marketing strategies you intend to use to reach your key customers and target market. It also illustrates how you intend to attract those consumers to your products, how you intend to sell to them, how you plan to price the product or service to make it attractive to the target audience, and everything else you do to drive the business to success.

Writing this part of the business plan demands that first, you research and know your target audience very well (which also means having a buyer persona ready). Without this understanding, and understanding of whom your marketing targets, it will be relatively difficult to have an effective marketing strategy.

A marketing plan has various other parts key of which are:

1. Positioning: Usually the first part of a marketing plan, this part details the things/activities/partnerships you will engage yourself in to position your business and products within the market. Essentially, positioning is about everything you should do to present your company/product in the best possible light to the target audience. Creating a positioning section requires a proper understanding of the current market and product offering, as well as how your product differs from the current offering. To create an effective marketing plan, consider how your competitors are positioning themselves, the strategies you intend to use to differentiate yourself, the customers primary pains, and how you intend to position yourself within the overall market. Like most of the other areas of the business plan, keep this part succinct.

2. Pricing: With your overall positioning strategy in place, you can then move on to the price section of the marketing plan. This part of the process involves detailing how you

intend to price your products and services; it heavily draws on your positioning strategy because how you intend to position yourself within the market will determine the prices of your products/services. We talked at length about pricing strategies—you can use cost-plus, market-based, or value pricing. Refer back to the chapter on pricing.

3. Promotion: Once you nail the pricing and positioning, create your promotion strategy where you detail how you intend to communicate with your targets and the various strategies you intend to use. Ensure that, because of its importance to the overall marketing plan, you can easily track the effectiveness of the different promotional strategies you choose to use. Areas that can be part of the promotional plan include packaging, i.e. the message communicated by your packaging as well as how it compares to the packaging offered by competitors advertising, which should include the advertising models you will use and how you intend to measure its effectiveness, and public relations, i.e. how you intend to manage your image. Other areas of promotion may include content marketing (especially important for online businesses) and a social media-marketing plan.

4. Key partnerships: Effective marketing is as much about the strategy as it is about the relationships you form with other strategic companies and businesses. Use this part of the marketing section to detail how you intend to form key partnerships with other businesses and companies that can give you access to the target market.

Operations

Operations is part of the marketing plan because it details how you will glue everything together and especially how the various parts of the business, be it the technology or the logistics, will work together to bring about the desired effect i.e. business profitability.

The business operations section of the business plan can have any of or all of the following subsections depending on the nature of the business (consider your business and determine what to keep and remove).

1. Sourcing and fulfillment: If you are sourcing your products from other vendors, use this section to detail where the product comes from, the delivery method used to get the products to you and then onwards to your target audience. Describe how you intend to deliver the goods and services to your target market and in cases where you intend to ship the goods to them, detail how you intend to do this in the most effective, cost-friendly manner.

2. Technology: Describe the pieces of technology you will use in your operations as well as how they influence the overall objective. While this section is especially important to technology businesses, it is still an important part of the marketing plan. The key is to ensure that if you have proprietary technology, you do not disclose too much of it. Relate the technology you have in play to how it helps you offer the best solution.

Distribution

This part is especially important to businesses that deal with physical products. It describes how you intend to get the product to retailers and onwards to consumers. The distribution channels you use will largely depend on your industry of operation. The most common types of distributions are direct and retail distribution. In direct distribution, you sell directly to the consumer. This method is relatively simple and the most profitable. In retail distribution, distribution companies get goods from different suppliers and then make the aggregated products available to retailers for a percentage of the sales.

Representatives (specifically manufacturer's representatives) are another great distribution channel because in most cases, these representatives often have cemented relationships with distributors and retailers, and are, therefore, a very effective way to ensure effective distribution of your products through the correct channels. Most of these representatives are commission-based.

You can use a variety of distribution channels; for instance, you can use both direct and retail distribution at the same time.

Metrics and milestones

How do you intend to actualize the plan? What kind of schedule will you follow? Who will do which role and what will be his or her responsibilities? Such are some of the key things you should include in the metrics and milestones part of the marketing plan.

Essentially, this part of the marketing plan should be simple and to the point. However, that does not mean it is not important. You should go out of your way to create a path for your business by creating milestones and metrics. Having this very important aspect of the business within the business plan shows investors (and anyone reading the business plan) that you understand what will happen, when and how you intend to move the business through the various steps that will take it to profitability.

Your milestones, the major business goals you have planned along the way, should come first: create a quick review of them. Milestones will vary depending on the type of business in question. For instance, a product company can have milestones such as creation of a prototype, testing, improvements, sourcing manufacturers, and taking to market.

Milestones and metrics are important because they show how you intend to drive your business forward. Traction is another important part of the overall milestones section that investors look at to determine how far you have come (your accomplishments). Examples of traction—proof that your business is viable—include significant partnerships, initial sales etc.

On metrics, you should include the elements you plan to keep a close eye on to determine if your business is on the route to profitability or success. These may include the key numbers you monitor to determine how your business is performing.

4: Business and people

The fourth section of the business plan, the business and people section, gives key details about the managerial structure adopted by your business as well as the people in key positions. These details are important to have in the business plan because it allows investors to know the people behind actualizing the business plan and driving the business forward.

The people/team

The team behind an idea is as important as the idea itself. Because the team you have behind you is central to the execution of your business idea, detailing who they are, their core skills and talents as well as their overall contribution to the success of the business can prove very central to drawing in investment.

Essentially, the aim of this part of the guide is to show investors that you have the right people rallied behind the business idea. This part of the document should include details of the people you have on your management team because those in these positions are central to the execution of the business idea.

Outlining this section in a most illustrative and clear manner shows that you know which person will be responsible for what and when as the business matures and grows into its own. Typical details to include in this part of the business plan include short bios of each key team member, their related experience and education background, and perhaps a brief description of why that person is the right person for that position.

Do not make the common mistake of describing your management team by giving all of them C-level titles because doing so is out of touch with reality because as your business grows, you will need differently skilled people and key team members.

As part of your business plan, you can include a command structure (proposed organizational chart) a plan of how you intend to organize people within the business. An organization chart (org chart for short) can be a very useful planning tool as your business enterprise grows.

The business

Also called a company overview, this part of the business plan includes your mission statement, intellectual property, the business ownership and legal structure, business location and history.

Keep the mission statement short and sweet: one or at most two sentences will do. Make sure it encompasses the very things your business stands for and is trying to do within the market.

Your ownership and legal structure is an important part of the business, which is why you should define it within the business plan. Is your business a partnership, an LLC, or a C or S-corporation? Define the legal structure succinctly.

5: Financial plan

The financial plan should be the last main chapter of your business plan. Most financial plans have a projection for the first 12 months of the business being in operation divided into individual months and then annual projections for 3-5 years.

A financial plan should include the following details:

1. Sales forecast: As the name suggests, a sales forecast is a projection of the amount of sales you predict to sell over a period. In most cases, the plan breaks down into several rows with each row representing an individual product or service.

2. Personnel plan: This part of the financial plan details how you plan to remunerate your employees, i.e. how much you intend to pay employees especially those in key positions. Your personnel plan should also include employee burden, which mean how much an employee costs the business after salary. Here, you will include things such as insurance, taxes, and any other expense accrued by employees within the month.

3. Income statement: Also called a profit and loss statement, this part of the document glues together the numbers you are working with to illustrate whether your business is turning a profit or taking in losses. Most P&L documents include sales, COGS (cost of goods sold), gross margin, operating expenses including total operating expenses, operating income, and net profit.

4. The cash flow statement: Unlike the P&L that calculates your overall profit or loss, the cash flow statement records the amount of liquid assets (cash at hand) you have at any point in time. This statement normally starts with the cash you have on hand, then details cash received and invoices paid and then minuses the cash you have paid out for bills, taxes, and any other expenses. The remainder is the total cash flow.

5. Balance sheet: The balance sheet shows investors the health of your business. It does so by detailing your assets, liabilities, and the equity of the business owner. To determine the worth of a company, investors deduct the company's liabilities from its assets.

6. Funds use: If you intend to seek investment, have a brief

section detailing how you intend to use the raised funds. Keep this section short and to the point.

7. Exit strategy: As part of your financial plan, include an exit strategy plan, a plan detailing how you intend to sell the business (eventually).

6: Appendix

While not an essential chapter, an appendix is useful to have within the business plan (as the last part of the business plan). In it, you can have charts, legal notes, and any other type of information you consider important or too long to include within the main business plan. For instance, you can include patents or illustrations of your products.

If you follow this plan, as detailed here, you should be able to create a very clear and actionable business plan that will act as a guide as you implement your business idea.

Now that your business plan is ready, the next thing we will discuss is how to develop a marketing plan for your business.

Chapter 18: How to Create a Marketing Plan for Your Business

Creating a marketing plan for your business is one of the most important steps to take to ensure that your business survives its first year.

Ever heard anyone say *"Advertising/marketing is the soul of business?"* Truer words have never been spoken- without shouting it out loud for people to see and hear, your business cannot really realize its full potential when it comes to sales. Yes, you might get people to buy from you every now and then, but trust me, your business can do better than that.

I've had people buy stuffs from me in the past and after the purchase, they say something like *"I wasn't going to buy this but because of the way you keep talking about it, I want to give it a try to see if it's as good as you say"*.

Marketing, when done the proper way, doesn't only bring you awareness; it also helps you break through the 'walls' of your potential clients/customers.

Unless you're selling foods, drugs, shelter, or things that people need for survival, you would have to do a good job of convincing them that they need to spend their money on what you're trying to sell to them because no one goes around thinking *"Hey, I got a couple of dollars to spend on random items"*.

And even if you're selling food, drugs or other must-haves, don't forget that there are dozens of brands that customers can easily choose from so you have to tell them why yours is the best option for them. How do you convince them that your product and your brand is the best for them?

Through marketing of course!

You can have the best product or service in the world but if you don't market it well, to its target market effectively, it cannot get far.

Do you see why marketing is the lifeblood of your business?

I know you get an idea of why marketing is the key to success in any business, big or small. It also explains why CocaCola, the world's biggest soft drinks manufacturer (and a household brand) is top on the list of companies with the biggest advertising budgets.

The truth is, just because you have a marketing budget does not mean you will succeed by magic; the marketing process of your business requires proper preparation, maybe even more than all the other aspects of the business. So how do you go about it to ensure you are successful? Well, the first thing you need to do is to assess your current situation. This is what is called a Situational Analysis.

Situational Analysis

You need to have a clear idea of what your business already has going for it as that would give you an idea of things that you'll need to put in place to ensure successful marketing.

Product and Service Description

Here, you have to make a list of the products and services that you're selling and what each product does.

For example, if I own a business that is into selling of

bathroom accessories, I'll make a list of all my products this way:

	Product/Service	Function
1	Non Slip Bathroom Mats	Helps to protect people from falling in the bathroom
2	Automatic Toothpaste Dispenser	Helps to save time when using toothpaste Helps to keep toothpaste tubs neatly stored in the bathroom

You must be able to describe your products and services, and what it's supposed to do for the people you plan to sell to- how each product or service is supposed to make their lives better.

Matching Product Features to Benefits

The next thing you have to do is to list the features of each product, and then write down the benefits of each feature. You must always bear in mind that what people are spending money on is the value that your product would add to them. Nobody cares about a bottle of water unless it is going to quench their thirst or perform some other magic that would improve their lives or wellbeing.

Therefore, you should be able to describe the features of your bottle of water and why customers should care about that. For instance, the size of the bottle is a feature e.g. 75cl bottle. So why should a customer care about a 75cl bottle? Well, this is simply because it's cheaper considering that other brands sell their 50cl bottles for the same price as what you're offering your 75cl bottle for.

So that's the benefit of the feature- customers get more value for their money!

Now we just have to expand the table that we created earlier to accommodate the features and benefits of all the products or services that you listed.

	Product/Service	Function	Product/Service Features	Product/Service Benefits
1	Non Slip Bathroom Mats	Helps to protect people from falling in the bathroom		
2	Automatic Toothpaste Dispenser	Helps to save time when using toothpaste Helps to keep toothpaste tubs neatly stored in the bathroom		

In case you're wondering why it's necessary to write down functions, benefits and features, this is why; because you need it for your demographic analysis, which is an essential part of your marketing plan.

Demographic Analysis

You would need to identify your target customers and this requires that you have an idea of people who would typically need the benefits of what you're selling.

Who would need a non-slip bathroom mat? Maybe parents with children, elderly people, etc.

Of course, there are other people who could need these products but these are probably people who would prioritize these things because it offers the most benefits to them.

Who would need an antibacterial non slip bathroom mat?

Make a list of people who would need your products/services, and narrow it down as much as possible.

You can use the table below to do a quick and easy demographic analysis.

Demographic Analysis	
Target Market	Who are those that typically require the benefits of your products?
Location	Where do they live? Which countries, cities, or towns do you plan to sell/ship your

	products and services to?
Age	How old do you think that people who require these products and services would be? 18-65? 25-40?
Sex	Are your products/services for men, women, or both sexes?
Marital Status	Do you want to sell to single or married people?
Family Structure	Are you targeting families of four, six, or larger families?
Educational level	Do you prefer to sell to College Graduates, High School Graduates or people who are more educationally advanced?
Race	Are you targeting whites, African-Americans, Hispanics, Asians, or others?

Why do you need a demographic analysis? It is simple; because not everyone is your customer and you can't afford to waste your marketing budget on people who are not going to buy from you.

If you're selling male shoes and your ads are targeting everyone, you're wasting too much money. Most advertising strategies today, especially digital-based strategies, allow you to target the exact type of customers that you are looking to buy from you and this helps to increase the success of your marketing campaign, while spending less money. You can decide to spend your money promoting your products or services to people who live in New York alone, or to females who live in New York alone.

Since you don't plan to sell to people who live in Connecticut, they would not get to see your ads and promotions and your money can be spent advertising to people who are likely to buy your products. If you have your demographic analysis done and written down somewhere, it's always easy to use it for marketing whenever you need to.

Next, our focus will be on competitive analysis to help you piece the whole puzzle together.

Chapter 19: Competitive Analysis

Your competitors are a threat to your business; they are there to take as many of your potential customers that they can for themselves. You both want the same things, which makes them a potential danger to your business because the survival of your business depends on your ability to do better than them, or at least convince your target customers that you're the better option.

This is why you cannot afford to ignore your competitors- your nose must always be in their businesses so that you can always stay ahead of them.

Identifying Direct and Indirect Competitors

Every business has both direct and indirect competitors, and both categories of competitors are potentially dangerous to your business.

- **Direct Competitors:** These businesses sell the exact same product as yours. For instance, if you sell wedding dresses, and the person on the next block also sells wedding dresses, that's a direct competitor.

- **Indirect Competitors**: Indirect competitors don't sell the same product as you but they can also steal potential customers away because they sell substitutes or alternatives to your products/services.

For instance, if there's a guy who offers wedding gown rental services in your area, that's an indirect competitor because potential customers can decide to rent a wedding dress from him instead of spending so much on a new wedding dress.

Identifying Competitive Advantage

The first thing to do is to identify, and make a list of your strongest competitors. This includes businesses operating in close proximity, businesses selling the same products/services as yours, and businesses selling the same products/services as you at cheaper rates than you are.

If you have more than 10 businesses on your list, you can narrow it down to 10 of your strongest competitors.

Next, write down the prices that they sell their products and services for and compare it to yours. You may need to do a bit of research for this.

- **Competitor's marketing strategies and methods**: You should also identify all the methods and strategies that these competitors are using to create awareness and visibility for their products- do they have a blog? Do they advertise on Facebook? Do they distribute their flyers in areas with heavy human traffic?

- **Competitor's Basic Objectives**: If you're a new or struggling business, this would give you a sense of direction as to how to approach your potential customers. Observe your competitor's marketing objectives closely to see what they are trying to achieve.

Are they trying to make their products cheaper? That probably means that the customers are more interested in cheaper products so you should also take the pricing aspect of your business very serious and seek for ways to make your prices even more competitive than theirs.

If it looks like your competitors are trying to target a new category of customers, you should look into that as well. For instance, if your competitor who sells tampons and sanitary pads is now trying to sell baby diapers, you should also look into that – diapers are probably a hot niche at the moment and you don't want to miss out on that.

- **Competitor's Marketing Strategies and Techniques**: Next, you have to look into the strategies and techniques that your competitors are using to create more awareness for their brand, and gain more customers. Are they doing Digital ad campaigns or television and radio advertising, flyers, Door to Door marketing?

- **Competitor's Weaknesses**: What do you think your competitor's should be doing that they are not doing? If you can identify any, that's a strength for you, and a weakness for them because you have a trick up your sleeve that they are not using, and you can use it to beat them, especially if it's a very brilliant one.

The goal is to look into what your competitors are doing, and do it better than them. You can also create a table (as shown below) so that it's easier for you to keep a track on your competitors.

	Your Direct Competitor	Your Indirect Competitor
Prices of Goods and Services • Product X • Product Y • Product Z		
Competitor's Marketing Strategies and methods		
Competitor's Basic Objectives		
Competitor's Current Marketing Strategies and Techniques		
Competitor's Weaknesses		

Now that you have a clear glimpse into your competitor's business strategies, you can use the information to make your business better. You have to make a list of the ways through which you can market better than your competitors do. This list that you make would form your marketing goals, and will be subsequently used to create a marketing budget for your business, which will be the subject of our discussion next.

Chapter 20: Creating Your Marketing Budget

Your Marketing Goals

After doing your situational analysis and your competitive analysis, you'll have a clearer idea of what your business has, and what it needs to do better.

So the first question you'll have to ask yourself here is *"How can I steal my competitor's customers for myself?"* Because the more of their customers you can convert to loyal customers of your business or brand, the more profit you'll earn.

So first, you must identify the following:

- The features and benefits of your products/services over those of your competitors: What are those features that are unique to your products/services and absent in those of your competition?

- What smart promotional strategies do you know about that your competitors are not using?

- Is there a way to slash your prices and make your products cheaper than your competitor's products?

- How can you make your products and services more appealing to your customers?

- How many units of products and services do you plan to sell daily/monthly/weekly, and how do you plan to make this a reality?

- Finally, what are the promotional strategies that you will use to make your products and services sell faster?

The answers to these questions will help to form your marketing goals.

Marketing Tactics and Strategies

Since you've done a demographic analysis and you know who your customers are, where they live, and their lifestyles, it's easier for you to choose your marketing strategies. You are able to tell which marketing strategies will appeal to your target customers better.

There are different types of marketing strategies that you can use including:

✓ **Paid Advertising**: You can create better awareness for your products and services with paid advertising. There are also different paid advertising strategies that you can use, depending on what works best for your target customers. You can decide to do:

  - Radio advertising

  - Distribution of flyers in high human traffic areas

  - Newspaper/Magazine ads placement

  - Display advertising e.g. billboards, banners, etc.

  - Door to door marketing.

  - Online advertising e.g. social media, digital marketing, online sponsored ads, search engine optimization, pay per click advertising, etc.

- Affiliate marketing (using affiliates to promote products and services)

✓ **Relationship Marketing**: This marketing strategy involves improving customer experience so that they can always come back for more, or recommend your products and services to other people.

✓ **Undercover Marketing**: You can choose to adopt subtle marketing strategies that wouldn't make it too obvious to your potential customers that you're trying to get them to buy what you're selling. For instance, you can set up a blog that helps to provide information, or teach them how to do some stuff and with that blog; you can subtly promote some of your products or services to potential customers.

✓ **Transactional Marketing**: Transactional marketing involves offering motivation to potential customers in form of discounts, coupons and value-added services, as a way to encourage them to patronize you.

Choose your preferred marketing strategy and then fill the table below so that you can have a clearer idea of the exact marketing strategies you want to use before you go on to create your marketing budget.

Type of Marketing Strategy	What are you trying to achieve with this marketing strategy?	Which methods do you plan to use? e.g. radio advertising, coupons, price slash, door to door marketing, etc.
Paid Advertising		
Transactional Marketing		
Undercover Marketing		
Relationship marketing		

Creating Your Marketing Budget

Preparing your marketing budget is the crux of everything that you've been doing so far. Your marketing strategies would cost you some money and you have to know just how much you would need. There are a lot of things that you would need to put into consideration before preparing your marketing budget.

For instance, you will need to consider 4 important factors:

✓ **People**: Who are the people that will help you carry out these marketing strategies? Will they be employees of your business or third party service providers? If they would be employees, will you need to train them for the job? How much will you have to pay them in salaries or commissions? What incentives will you give them to motivate them to perform better?

✓ **Distribution Network**: How do you plan to get your

goods across to your customers? Will you need a brick-and-mortar store or a delivery van to improve delivery? How much will it cost?

✓ **Promotion**: What are the promotional methods that you plan to use and how much will it cost you?

✓ **Branding**: How will you separate your products and services from all the others in the market? How much will it cost you to brand your business?

When you have all the answers to these questions, you would already have your marketing budget because you already know what you need to achieve your marketing goals, and how much it would cost you.

All that is left to do is to make a list of everything you plan to do, and put the cost in front of it- that's your marketing budget.

But if you would like something more formal, you can use a marketing budget template to create your marketing budget. You can find many templates online for free.

With all that in mind, let's take our discussion a little deeper into discussing how to manage operations.

Part 6: Operations Management

Chapter 21: Introduction to Operations Management

What is Operation Management?

Every business has its unique set of operations. Operations refer to how a business creates its output- products and services, and how it ensures that the goods and services get to the customers so that the customers are happy with their experiences when they do business with a business organization.

Operations management involves proper planning, organization and supervision of all the processes involved in the business operations in order to increase the business's profitability, and ensure that the goals of the business are met.

Operations management is crucial to the success of every business because it helps to increase productivity, and helps you manage business resources more efficiently so that you can avoid wastage and avoidable businesses expenses.

Basically, operations management helps you plan, and make judicious use of your business resources.

Operations management helps you understand;

- The operational process- Every single activity involved from production to end-user supply. And by understanding the operational process, you'll be able to figure out:

- The raw materials and resources that will be required to produce each unit, and get it to the end-user.

- The processes and people that will be involved from production to end-user supply.

And when you know these, you'll be able to:

- Allocate a budget to each process.

- Figure out ways and areas where you can cut costs.

The Functions and Importance of Operations Management

- **Product or Service Management:** Operations management helps you understand how to improve your products and services and how to develop new products/services ideas so that your business always offers the best experience to customers, and stays on top of trends. For instance, if there's a product line that needs to be discontinued because it is bringing losses to the company, operations management will help you notice the losses quickly and decide the next course of action to take. In this case, you would know whether to discontinue the product/service altogether, or replace the product/service with a more profitable alternative before any damage is done to your business.

- **Customer Experience Management**: Operations management helps you understand how customers feel about your products and services at every point in time. If there is anything your customers are not happy about, you'll notice it quickly and before it does too much damage to your business.

- **Human Resources Management**: Another thing that operations management helps with is to manage your employees and human capital efficiently. It helps to ensure that you are not over-staffed or under-staffed, and every person you hire is contributing to the overall growth and profitability of your business. It also helps you to keep an eye on the salaries and wages that you're paying to your employees so that you can be sure that you're not over-rewarding them to the detriment of your business, or paying them too little such that they are not motivated enough to put in their best.

- **Facility Management**: Facility management is another aspect of operations management. Facility management is simple enough- you want all your business facilities managed properly so that they can depreciate slowly, and have a longer useful life.

- **Inventory Control**: You don't want to hold too much or too little inventory because whilst the latter causes you to lose customers and revenues, holding too much inventory constitutes a waste of business resources.

The Essential Qualities of an Operations Manager

Operations management is a serious aspect of business that must be entrusted in the hands of qualified and experienced professionals with the required qualities and skills because the success or failure of your entire business operations rests on the ability of this individual to do a good job.

You can choose to be the operations manager for your business- there are no rules against that, as long as you can afford the time and you have the required skills and qualities.

But whether you choose to do it yourself, or hire a business operations manager, you must ensure that the person doing the job has the necessary skills and qualities to succeed.

Some essential qualities of a good operations manager include:

- **Must be Realistic and Proactive**: Your operations manager must always be realistic about the goals and challenges of the business. Challenges and potential problems must never be swept under the carpet until it boomerangs. Managers must be able to troubleshoot and see potential problems before they happen. Managers must also be proactive and find solutions to challenges as they occur.

- **Must Prioritize Quality**: Quality products and quality service delivery must be more important to an operations manager than cutting of costs. Every business wants to spend less money and earn more but an operations manager must never jeopardize quality in order to cut costs.

- **Must be good with Decision Making**: Being an operations manager involves a lot of decision making, especially under pressure. A good one must be able to think on his feet and make good decisions even under pressure.

- **Must be a Good Leader**: A good operations manager must also know how to lead the employees and human assets of the business well. He must understand the difference between being a boss and being a leader.

- **Must Know How to Manage Business Resources Judiciously**: The whole point of operations management is so that the business resources can be used efficiently.

Chapter 22: Facets of Operations Management

Inventory Management

Inventory holding ties a lot of your business capital down hence the need for solid inventory management.

Your inventory management system must focus on ways to:

- **Avoid Spoilage**: If you're selling products that can expire or products that can go bad or stale (like food and fruits), you must embrace a good inventory management system that helps you avoid spoilage.

- **Reduce Storage Costs**: The more inventory you stock, the more the costs of storage e.g. warehousing, lighting and heating, refrigeration, theft prevention, etc. You must think of ways to reduce inventory and storage costs for your business.

- **Prevent Dead Stock**: Some items can go out of style or out of season. This is especially true for people doing business in the fashion industry. You must figure out ways to avoid getting caught up with outdated stocks that constitute losses for the business.

- **Improve Cash Flow**: There are a lot of areas of your business where you can use the extra cash rather than tie it up in slow-moving goods. You should think about inventory management techniques that help you improve business cash flow.

Here are some helpful inventory management ideas you can

use:

- **Determine and Set Par Levels**: You should set 'par levels' for each of your products. Par levels refer to the minimum amount of a particular product that is safe to have on hand at all times based on how quickly the item sells, and how much time it takes to restock. With this technique, you'll only restock when items are needed, and you'll avoid keeping too much stock on hand.

- **Use First-in-First-Out (FIFO) Method of Stock Control**: The FIFO method of stock control is a good system to minimize spoilage or dead stock. The technique involves selling out your oldest stock first before displaying new ones to your customers.

- **Maintain Good Relationships With Suppliers**: When you have a good relationship with your suppliers, it's easier to restock sold-out products and sometimes, you can even negotiate minimum order quantities so that you can restock more often, and with ease. This knocks out the need for excess storage.

- **Contingency Planning**: You should always plan for things like unexpected spikes in sales, miscalculations, slow-moving products, sudden increases in prices, and other problems that may be caused by your supplier.

- **Regular Auditing**: There are computer programs that you can use to manage inventory but you must also conduct regular audits of your inventory to prevent pilferage and losses.

Supply Chain Management

Your business must run seamlessly at all times and that means that you must always have control over all the activities involved, from the purchase of the products from the supplier, through to the distribution to the final consumers- all the processes involved must run seamlessly.

This requires a lot of planning.

Aspects such as demand planning, raw material sourcing or product sourcing, manufacturing, quality control management, inventory management, storage, logistics and transportation must be pre-planned in a step by step basis, and monitored.

There are computer programs that can be used for effective supply management but if you run a small business or cannot afford such programs, you can simply write down all the processes involved in executing a business transaction, and map out an effective system that allows everything to run seamlessly such that customers are always satisfied after every transaction. This also ensures your business resources are used to generate the highest amounts of profits possible on each transaction.

Delivery Management

If you run a business that involves transferring products or deliverables from one location to the other, delivery management is an essential aspect of your business because you want to ensure that:

- Products get to customers in a timely manner. We live in a fast-paced world where people are generally impatient and want items that they paid for to be delivered to them as quickly as possible. This is especially true for online-based businesses and businesses that deliver the fastest are believed to be the most customer-centric.

- Delivery is cost-efficient. You want to ensure that the method of delivery that you adopt is not only cost-efficient for you but for the customers as well.

- Returns are properly arranged for. What if the customer doesn't like an item after it gets to them; how does it get sent back to you in a way that doesn't hurt you or your customer?

- Return policies are established- how many days will you allow for returns? What are the conditions and procedures for returns?

- Deliveries can be tracked both by you and your customers.

- Contingencies are planned for-accidents; a driver takes off with goods to be delivered, goods get damage in transit, etc.

Quality Control Management

Your business is only as good as the quality of your products and services. If your customers are satisfied with what they get from you, they would come back and even bring other people with them and in the same vein, if you offer them bad products or unsatisfactory services, they won't only stop doing business with you, they would also spread the word to others.

So your business must be hands-on with quality control and that means that you must:

- Ensure that your business always deliver as promised. Don't advertise what you cannot offer. If you've told them that your product would end their headache, be sure that it can do just that. If you've told them you're offering them two items for the price of one, don't ship one item to them. It doesn't matter if the customers will complain or not- you must always protect the reputation of your business by offering whatever you promise at all times.

- Establish a good feedback management system. It's always better when customers can bring their grievances to you first. I was searching for hotels for my vacation once and saw photos of a really nice hotel. I was sold out on that hotel until I decided to check reviews online and found a third-party review platform with dozens of customers saying ugly stuff about the hotel. They complained about everything from the food to the size of the bed. For a customer to take the time to go on a third party platform to leave nasty reviews about a company, then they must have been really pissed and felt the need to complain to somebody. But let's say the hotel had a complaints box or a complaint's form somewhere on their website, then maybe customers would have been able to let the company know about their disappointments before sharing it with the world. The company would also be able to use the feedbacks to improve their service delivery.

- **Good Customer Support System**: You should also establish a good customer support system for your business so that when customers need help, tips, or need to make enquires, they can always find the help that they need.

Operating Cost Management

When you first start a business, your costs will likely be very high but eventually, it can start to reduce. This is what is called a learning curve. As you continue to run the business, you'll become privy to some knowledge, tips and secrets that would help you cut costs. But you should never leave this to chance. A good operations manager must go after cost control measures rather than wait for it to land on his laps. This means that on every business transaction, you must never leave a dollar on the table.

If your delivery company has agreed to a $35 flat shipping rate nationwide, and you have an order that needs to be shipped within the city, by all means negotiate with them and see if they can reduce the shipping rates on that transaction so that you can rake in higher profits.

If you're ordering for more products than you often do, don't hesitate to renegotiate with your supplier and see if they can slash prices a bit further. These are examples of ways to be proactive with operating cost control.

The most important thing however is that for every day that your business is open for transaction, cost control should always be of paramount importance, must be approached proactively, and must never be done in a way that affects product or service quality.

Next, we will look at another aspect that will ultimately improve your bottom line i.e. your online presence.

Part 7: Marketing In Today's Environment

Chapter 23: Creating a Website or a Blog for Your Business

Why You Need a Website

No matter what you sell, your business can always benefit from having an online presence. Many more people are embracing internet use these days and according to recent statistics, around 90% of Americans use the internet to search for local businesses and services.

So instead of asking the next door neighbor for directions to the pet store, most people just pick up their phones or computers to search for addresses online.

Now imagine that potential customers can find you easily, determine whether you're open or closed for business, establish credibility by reading through reviews from previous customers, send photos of your products or executed jobs to their friends and acquaintances while trying to convince them to do business with you or even connect with other customers via your businesses' social media pages.

There are a lot of benefits that you can enjoy when you take your business online. In addition, according to future projections, brick-and-mortar businesses are likely to go extinct in the nearest future- that means that your business may become irrelevant in the nearest future should you refuse to embrace the online business model. You would have a lot to gain and nothing to lose from running your business both online and offline.

There are a couple of steps involved in setting up an online presence for your business but it starts with creating a website.

And guess what? Far gone are the days when you had to spend thousands of dollars to get a website for your business. These days, you can get a standard professional website for your business for $100 or less (depending on the features you want) on freelancing platforms like Fiverr.com, Upwork.com, or Freelancer.com.

And if you're not in the mood to spend money on a website, you can create one yourself- it's now easier than it used to be in the past. I found this beginner tutorial helpful for setting up a website two months ago- *easy peasy and not in the least bit rocket science-y*! I'm sure you would find it helpful too.

Let me take the discussion a bit further to ensure you start well and catapult yourself to success.

Tips for Building Effective Business Websites

Whether you choose to have a professional build your website for you or you choose to set it up by yourself, there are a few things you must put in place for your website to achieve its aim. Have you ever tried to visit a website only for it to load very sluggishly that you had to abandon it and look for a better alternative? No matter what you are selling, you will have competitors who would most likely have websites too so for every time your website fails to load fast, you lose a potential customer.

So your business website must be designed in such a way that it loads super-fast- this means that the theme and design must not be too bulky.

Some other tips for building effective business websites

include:

- Websites should be mobile-friendly: That means that the website must be able to load seamlessly on a mobile device just as it would on a computer because a good number of people access the web from their phones these days.

- Must be Clutter Free and Easy to Navigate: If potential customers cannot find what they are looking for easily, they'll leave. So avoid packing too much information on your website, and use a layout that allows people to find what they are looking for easily.

- Must have contact details that are very easy to find. The whole point of having a business website is so that people can find and connect with you easily. So make sure you make it easy for them to connect with you by making your contact details visible.

- Brand Your Website: Customers should be able to identify your website with your business, and differentiate it from those of your competitors. Consider using unique themes, banners, and backgrounds that are unique and represent your business.

- Showcase your products and services well and don't assume that people know what your business is about- explain the features and the benefits of your business to them in details.

Why Create a Blog?

Most people who visit the internet are looking for two things- entertainment or information. And the best way to catch their attention and create more awareness for your products and services is by using these two tools.

Your business website is like a business card that carries just the basic information about your business but with a blog, you can share a lot more with your customers, connect with them better, and convince them to do business with you.

Content Ideas for Business Blogs

The types of articles that you would publish on your blog would of course depend on the nature of your business but for a start, here are a few article ideas that work for most businesses.

- Customer success stories i.e. expanded testimonials.

- Frequently Asked Questions: Create a long post with answers to some of the most popular questions/challenges that customers in your niche usually have.

- New trends in the industry

- How-to posts- Teach your customers how to do some things themselves, especially things that would help them save some money.

- Product or service reviews. Review products or services that your customers may like.

- Comparison posts. Compare products and services.

- Video posts. Video tutorials, sneak previews of new products, promotions and event recaps.

- Infographic posts

- Behind the scene posts- how your products are made or

procedures for service delivery.

- Explainer articles or videos- teach them how to use your products and services.

- Create Contests or Giveaway posts.

- Tell a story about how your business started, how you got the idea, the challenges on the way, etc.

- Create articles similar to those of your competitors.

- Tips and tricks.

- Interview a celebrity or authority in the industry.

- Create inspirational posts.

The discussion on marketing would be incomplete in today's world without a discussion on social media marketing. That's why it will be the subject of our discussion next.

Chapter 24: Social Media Marketing

Did you know that 75% of male internet users and 83% of female internet users are also users of Facebook? Or that 22% of the world's total population use Facebook? This tells you that the fastest way to get everyone to notice your products or business is to put it on Facebook because obviously, that's where everyone hangs out these days.

From senior citizens to teenagers, you'll find all age groups, races, income groups and other demographic classes on Facebook and not just on Facebook but on other social media platforms including, Instagram, Twitter, Pinterest, Snapchat, and so many others. This is why businesses are not approaching their social media marketing efforts with kid's gloves, and you shouldn't either. Let's discuss more about marketing on different social media platforms.

Facebook Marketing

With Facebook's huge user base, you can use it to attract new customers, and maintain contact with your existing customers. Whether you're a big brand or a small business, you can always benefit from Facebook marketing. So how do you go about it?

How to Develop a Facebook Marketing Campaign

- **A Dedicated Facebook Page:** First, you'll need to create a dedicated page for your business on Facebook.

  It's really easy to create one and your teenage niece can do it but if you are too busy to do it yourself, you can engage the services of experts to do it for you. You can find someone from Fiverr.com, Upwork.com, Freelancer.com, Guru.com etc. Make sure you brand your page- use a profile and cover photo that represents your brand. If you still want to create your own page but don't know how to go about it, you can refer to this guide: https://buffer.com/library/how-to-create-manage-facebook-business-page

- **Link Your Facebook Page to Your Blog**: You must link your Facebook page with your blog so that you can cross-promote- you can send customers from your Facebook page to your blog, encourage them to share your blog posts on their own social media pages, and also direct traffic from your blog to your social media account.

- **Create Some Infotainment**: Remember that Facebook is first a social media platform before anything else so don't make your page too 'serious'. I mean, don't be boring. Your posts must always be entertaining as they are informative.

- **Use Facebook Ads**: While you can advertise on your page for free, you can generate even more traffic and sales when you use paid advertising on Facebook. The best thing about paid ads on Facebook is that you are allowed to target specific demographics so that you get more value for your money.

Believe me; I have never seen a marketing campaign that converts as much as Facebook Marketing does. You can link your ads to your sales page, product page, Facebook page, and your blog or opt-in page for your email marketing campaign.

Well, setting up a successful marketing campaign on Facebook can be challenging for a beginner. To ensure you start well, you can refer to the resources below:

https://www.socialmediaexaminer.com/facebook-ads-facebook-advertising-guide-for-marketers/

https://www.disruptiveadvertising.com/social-media/facebook-ads-guide/

- **Host Facebook Contests**: This always works for attracting new likes or followers to your Facebook page. You can host a contest on your page and ask your existing subscribers to participate and ask their friends to subscribe to your page for a chance to win. You can gain more fans and increase awareness for your brand with this.

- **Promote Your Posts**: Facebook also allows you to promote your posts for a small fee. This is another way to boost engagement and gain more followership for your Facebook page.

Instagram Marketing

Instagram marketing is much similar to Facebook page except for the fact that Instagram is more glamour-themed. If you want to see who just bought the coolest ride, or who owns the most designer shoes, Instagram is the place to go. This is what makes Instagram slightly different from Facebook; you can't afford to be boring on Instagram- for people to engage with you, your posts must be interesting.

So how do you go about it?

Just like Facebook marketing, you need to create a dedicated business account on Instagram and cross-promote between your blogs and Instagram posts. Instagram also allows you to share your posts on your Facebook page so you don't have to create separate posts for your social media accounts- just create one post and share it across all other social media accounts.

Here are some effective ways to use Instagram for social media marketing:

- **Post Short Videos**: You can put up interesting videos on Instagram to keep your followers. The more interesting your Instagram page is, the more audience you'll get.

- **Use Social Media Influencers**: One marketing strategy that always works on Instagram is the use of social media influencers. Social media influencers are usually celebrities or people with a large social media following. These people can help you drive traffic to your business, or help you gain more audience when you pay them to talk about your business on their pages.

- **Riding on Popular Hashtags**: Hashtags will give your business lots of free publicity if you use them consistently so be sure to use popular hashtags, which relate to your niche. This perhaps explains why Instagram posts with at least one hashtag generate 12.6% more engagement than those without. You can refer to this comprehensive guide on hashtags:

  https://blog.hubspot.com/marketing/instagram-hashtags

- **Use Instagram Sponsored Posts**: Just like Facebook, Instagram also allows you put up paid ads, and target specific demographics and yes, it converts well too.

YouTube and Video Marketing

Most businesses think social media marketing ends with Facebook, Instagram but what they do not realize is that YouTube is one of the most widely used social networks in the world. People watch more than 5 billion videos on YouTube daily.

If you search for something on Google search engine, it's not uncommon to see a couple of videos pop up amongst the search engine results- that's a gold mine that many people neglect. If you include YouTube marketing to your social media marketing campaign, you would have a chance to stay ahead of your competition.

So how do you use YouTube for marketing?

- **Create a YouTube account and Channel**: As usual, you would have to create and customize a dedicated YouTube page for your business.

- **Upload Engaging Videos**: You have to create engaging videos that would attract the kind of audience that you are looking for to your page.

    Here are a few helpful ideas:

    ✓ Product Spotlights- create a video about the features, and how to use your products.

    ✓ Products in action- videos showing your products in action.

    ✓ Product explanation- how to use your products.

- ✓ Infographics

- ✓ New collections or releases – show them your new products or collections.

- ✓ Customer testimonials

- ✓ How-to Videos- helpful tutorials and various topics.

- ✓ Promotions and special offers

- ✓ Adverts

- ✓ Customer stories

- ✓ Behind the scenes videos

- ✓ Business/company milestones

- ✓ Tips and Tricks

- ✓ Discussions –Talk about news, trends, controversies, correct some misconceptions, etc.

- ✓ Contests- encourage followers to create videos for a chance to win gifts, and then post them on your channel and ask your audience to select winners.

- ✓ Inspirational videos

- ✓ A day in your life- let your audience get to know you better; it helps build trust.

- ✓ Funny Videos

- **Use Keywords in Your Descriptions**: You will be allowed to write a short description for each of your videos and that's a good chance to optimize your videos for better search engine visibility so that your videos can also pop up in search engine results.

What you should do is to add keywords to your video descriptions so that both YouTube users and non-YouTube audience can find your videos and channel easily. You'll see your traffic and engagement go through the roof when you do this.

- **Use Call-to-Actions**: Remember that you're not just doing YouTube marketing to entertain people; you're doing it as a way to generate more revenues and profit for your business hence your videos must always have a call-to-action. Do you want them to visit your blog, buy a product, or share the posts with their friends? Make sure to mention what you want your audience to do. Your video posts must always have a purpose and a target that must be included in your call to action.

- **Include Blog or Website URLs in Your Posts:** Always encourage your YouTube followers to visit your blog or website so that they can learn more about your business. Never, ever leave a chance to cross-promote on the table.

- **Embed Your YouTube Videos in Your Blog Posts**: Another effective way to use YouTube marketing is to embed your YouTube videos in your blog posts. This ensures that when people are reading through your blog posts, they can see the videos and visit your YouTube channel, subscribe, and become regular visitors to your YouTube channel.

Here are two comprehensive guides on how to get started with

YouTube marketing if you want to learn more:

https://www.hubspot.com/youtube-marketing

https://blog.hootsuite.com/youtube-marketing/

When you employ all three social media marketing strategies mentioned in this chapter, you'll have a greater chance of attracting all categories of internet users to your page. For people who love to read stuff, you have your blog posts. For those who love photos, there's Instagram and Facebook. And for those who prefer videos, you have your YouTube channel. In simple terms, there's something for everyone!

Now that we have a website, blog and social media accounts set up, how exactly are you going to make people to visit your pages so that you can engage them and perhaps convert them to regular readers and customers? Let's discuss traffic generation in the next chapter.

Chapter 25: Traffic Generation

You have a website. You have a blog with great content. And you have social media pages for your business too. But all of those will go to waste if you don't have enough people visiting those pages and engaging with your posts. Traffic generation is a way to direct more people to read your posts, visit your blogs and buy your products and services.

Generating more traffic will help you to achieve 2 main things:

- **Increase Sales**: Because the more people you have visiting your website, blog or social media pages, the more opportunities you have to advertise your offerings to them and get them to buy from you.

- **Improves Visibility**: Traffic generation helps to improve visibility for your website and blog posts so that more people can see them.

In this chapter, we'll discuss three of the most important and effective traffic generation strategies that you should use for your business.

Search Engine Optimization

We've talked about Search Engine Optimization briefly and by now you already understand that it involves making your pages more visible on the internet so that people who are searching for related products, services, or topics can find your website/blog easily.

Search Engine Optimization is a very wide subject and most businesses employ SEO experts to do it for them but there are some basics that you can handle yourself.

- **Keyword Research:** Search Engine Optimization starts with keyword research. You must first know what people are interested in, and what words they are typing into their search boxes to find those topics.

  There are a number of free and paid software that you can use to do keyword research for your blog like the Google Keyword Planner, KWFinder, SERPStat, LongTailPro, and SEMRUSH. These softwares will tell you which keywords are most suitable for your business and your niche.

- **Keywords in Content:** It doesn't stop with learning the keywords; you also have to cleverly put them in between your articles and blog posts and even in your social media posts. Where it becomes technical is that you have to use the keywords in a way that will make sense.

  So, if for instance, the keyword is 'Dog Groomers Houston' you cannot alter in your articles to make more sense; you will have to use it that way. It's called SEO writing and there are freelance writers who offer this as a professional service on Freelancing platforms like Upwork.com, Fiverr.com, Guru.com, Freelancer.com and many others.

- **Great Titles:** When good keywords help your web pages pop up on the front page of search engine results, your titles will determine whether people visit your page or not. Make sure your titles are captivating. They can be shocking, spark curiosity, answer questions- just make sure the title make people want to take a look at what is on your web page.

- **Other SEO Tips:** Like I stated earlier, SEO is a broad topic and if I wanted to teach you all about SEO, I would need all the pages in this book to do so. However, the tips in this book are a good place to start.

Some of the other helpful SEO tips that I have not mentioned include:

✓ **Write Long Posts:** It is a common belief in the SEO industry that our brothers over at Google (the biggest search engine), and in fact all search engines prefer long posts because it is believed that longer posts offer more information for their users. Some people would argue that lengths of posts don't matter but from personal experience, I think longer posts make your web pages friendlier to search engines.

✓ **Use Images:** Yes, images work too because people relate to visuals better than words. So don't forget to use a good photo, graph, or infographics in your posts wherever relevant.

✓ **Update Regularly:** Don't upload contents today and go AWOL for weeks. Search engines love pages with more activity especially up-to-date contents. So if you post today, and abandon your page for months, it is believed that your contents would be stale and that pushes your page further down the search engine scales.

Lead Generation/Email Marketing

Another aspect of traffic generation is lead generation.

I love how Wikipedia defines it; simple and easy to grasp the entire concept.

Lead generation is the initiation of customer interest or enquiry into products or services of a business.

It is a way to attract people who are searching for related products and services to your page and convert them into subscribers or followers so that you can always promote your services and products to them continuously.

There are four elements of Lead Generation:

o **Lead Capture**: Most times, visitors to your web pages are one-time visitors. Maybe search engines brought them to your page whilst they were searching for something and the odds are that they will never return to your page unless of course they really like your pages or need something you're selling. But there's a way to make them regular visitors to your page and that is by encouraging them to leave their emails with you so that you can reach out to them regularly- inform them when you have new posts on your blog, let them know about sales offers, new products, and so on.

o **Lead Magnet**: However, people will not leave their emails easily unless you have something to offer. So what you should do is to prepare a gift- maybe a book, software, discounts and coupons, or some other free gifts that you can offer them in exchange for their email addresses.

o **Landing Pages**: You would also need a landing page, which is also called an opt-in page. Your landing page is where you tell your visitors about the benefits that they will get when they leave you their emails- all the interesting things they will learn, the discounts they will get, how they will be the first to learn about your new products and services, and so on.

Your landing page will also have information about your lead magnet. So basically, you'll tell them "Leave me your email and get this for free". Not in those exact words but that's the information you need to pass across to them. There are a lot of templates that you can use to create landing pages easily on the internet- search for a nice, neat and attractive one in your templates/plug-in stores and add it to your website or blog.

o **Automation**: You can't sit behind your computer all day engaging with every new subscriber; hence, you will need a tool that helps you automate the process. So you need a tool/software that helps you engage with your subscribers regardless of whether you are there or not.

For that, you'll need automation tools called Autoresponders. With an Autoresponder, you can even upload everything you want to send to your subscribers for a year and determine what dates and times you want to send them in, and the rest is done for you easily.

Affiliate Marketing

Another effective way to drive traffic to your website and generate more sales for your business is by using a strategy called affiliate marketing. Affiliates are usually bloggers, people with large email lists, or people with a lot of subscribers and followers on social media.

These people already have the traffic that you are looking for so what you do is to tell them *"Hey, I would offer you some commission for every sale you make or every potential customer you send my way if you advertise my business to your audience"*.

Affiliate marketing is neglected by many business owners but it's a very powerful marketing too.

And you know the best part? You don't have to pay them for their services- they only get paid when you see results. So, no sales means no commission.

If you didn't include affiliate marketing in your marketing strategy that you wrote earlier, you should go back and include it because it's very effective especially for driving sales.

And no, affiliate marketing is not only for online-based businesses- it works for all types of businesses

Where to Find Affiliates for Your Business

Affiliates are very easy to find. You can find them in the following places:

- **Affiliate Networks**: There are platforms that are specially designed for companies to meet affiliates who can help them promote their products.

  Some of the most popular affiliate networks include Share-A-Sale, ClickBank, and Commission Junction (CJ).

- **Referrals**: For local businesses, you can ask for referrals from businesses that also use affiliates in your town or city.

- **Facebook Groups:** There are lots of Facebook groups for affiliates. Just type a related keyword in your Facebook search engine and you'll be able to find some of those groups and connect with affiliates.

Next, we will be discussing something very important; entrepreneurial mindset.

Part 8: The Entrepreneurial Mindset

Chapter 26: How to Develop the Entrepreneurial Mindset

One of the reasons why some people fail in business while some others succeed and have their businesses handed down to generations and generations of family members is because the first group of people- those who are failing in business, lack something called The Entrepreneurial Mindset.

Quitting your job to follow your passion does not make you an entrepreneur. Neither does investing your savings in an attractive business opportunity.

What makes you an entrepreneur, a successful entrepreneur, is your mindset- whether you have the entrepreneurial mindset or not.

What is the Entrepreneurial Mindset?

"An entrepreneur is a problem seeker, a problem solver, and an innovator. I don't think entrepreneurship is limited to those who start organizations or ventures. More than anything, an entrepreneur is a person that can add value, whether they create something themselves or work for a company." Mark Greenberg

The entrepreneurial mindset is a set of traits and characteristics that sets you apart, and drives your success as an entrepreneur. It is what separates a moneybag with lots of capital to invest from a person who knows how to build businesses and make it work.

If you have the entrepreneurial mindset, you don't necessarily need to have a lot of capital to work with; with just few resources at your disposal, you can build multiple businesses from the ground up and they would all be a success.

Mark Greenberg of BuildEd defines three components of the entrepreneurial mindset.

- The ability to identify opportunities or problems that need to be solved.

- The ability to create value and solve problems in a unique way that stands out from what everyone else is doing.

- Monetize that value- make money from providing value and solving problems.

So how exactly do you develop an entrepreneurial mindset? We will discuss some helpful tips on how to do that.

Tips for Growing an Entrepreneurial Mindset

- **Find Customers First**: An entrepreneur doesn't pursue ideas first and look for market later. This means that before you invest in any business or product idea, you must first test the idea and see if it's a viable one, and ascertain that there's a market for it first.

- **Always Find New Markets for Existing Products/Services**: Entrepreneurs are never satisfied with current results- you must always bear in mind that there is opportunity for growth always.

- **Network to Build Your Business**: You must understand that people are your greatest assets and you must use your human assets judiciously and that includes your mentors, existing customers, friends, local celebrities, suppliers, and everyone that can contribute to advancing your business.

- **Accept Failures**: Entrepreneurs understand that failures are integral parts of business growth and they are learning opportunities not roadblocks.

- **Take Risks**: Business is all about risk taking after all. However, an entrepreneur must understand the difference between smart risks and foolish ones. You must be able to identify and take smart risks to advance the course of your business.

- **Never Lose Sight of Your Vision**: The only time some entrepreneurs regard their business visions is when they are writing their business plans. After that, they forget all about it. Your vision statement describes your long-term plans for your business-the reason why you set up the business in the first place. Hence, you must always keep it in mind and consider it when making important business decisions.

- **Understand the Power of Branding and Rebranding**: Your business must always stand out from all other businesses in a unique and attractive way. You must also understand that branding is not a one-time thing. You should rebrand your business often as your business grows.

- **Find out What Works for Your Business:** Trends are a dime a dozen these days, and you can lose direction if you decide to follow every trend, strategy and business method out there. A good entrepreneur finds out what works for their business and sticks with it regardless of what everyone else is doing.

- **Always Maintain Quality Control**: We already discussed this when we were talking about operations management. Quality must be prioritized over extra profit at all times.

- **Lead, Don't Boss**: This is very important. An entrepreneur must know how to lead a team and stir them towards success in a way that makes them want to go the extra mile for your business and ensure growth and success rather than resent you or working for you.

Conclusion

I hope this book gave you the push to go out there and start that business you have been putting off. Take the risk. It is better to try and fail than not try at all. Failure is part of success. A life of regret because you did not try is not something you want.

After reading this book, I urge you to apply what you have learned because only through the application of knowledge and wise thoughts can you get result. Most people know what to do but they do not do what they know which is not good. Be a doer; after all, actions speak louder than words.

If you know anyone you think may be interested in this book or could benefit from what you have read here, please send them the link to this book. Please also leave an honest review on Amazon so that more people can see this book.

Best of luck in your entrepreneurial journey and always remember that you can do anything you set your mind to.

Printed in Great Britain
by Amazon